Deleuze

Edited by

Sandra Buckley

Michael Hardt

Brian Massumi

Theory out of Bounds

Deleuze

The Clamor of Being

Alain Badiou

Translated by Louise Burchill

Theory out of Bounds   *Volume 16*

University of Minnesota Press

Minneapolis • London

The University of Minnesota Press gratefully acknowledges
financial assistance provided by the
French Ministry of Culture for the translation of this book.

First published in France as *Deleuze: La clameur de l'Etre*.
Copyright 1997 by Hachette Littératures.

Excerpts from *Difference and Repetition*, by Gilles Deleuze, translated by Paul Patton.
Copyright 1994 by Columbia University Press.
Reprinted with permission of the publisher.

Excerpts from *The Logic of Sense*, by Gilles Deleuze, translated by Mark Lester
with Charles Stivale. Copyright 1990 by Columbia University Press.
Reprinted with permission of the publisher.

Excerpt from *Cinema 1: The Movement-Image*, by Gilles Deleuze, translated by
Hugh Tomlinson and Barbara Habberjam. Copyright 1986 Athlone Press.
Reprinted courtesy of The Athlone Press.

Published by the University of Minnesota Press
111 Third Avenue South, Suite 290
Minneapolis, MN 55401-2520
http://www.upress.umn.edu

LIBRARY OF CONGRESS CATALOGING-IN-PUBLICATION DATA
Badiou, Alain.
[Deleuze. English]
Deleuze : the clamor of being / Alain Badiou ; translated by
Louise Burchill.
p.   cm. — (Theory out of bounds ; v. 16)
Includes bibliographical references and index.
ISBN 978-0-8166-3140-7

1. Deleuze, Gilles.   I. Title.   II. Series.
B2430.D454B3513   1999
194 — dc21
99-41281

UMP LSI

Contents

Contents

Translator's Preface: Portraiture in Philosophy, or Shifting Perspectives

Louise Burchill

IT IS sufficiently rare for an important philosopher to devote a book—especially one unable to be classified simply as commentary or critique—to one of his contemporaries, that, when Gilles Deleuze published his text on Michel Foucault in 1986,[1] two years after Foucault's death, the question that incessantly returned in the reviews of the book and in the interviews with the author was that of the reason prompting the undertaking as such. Was one to understand the book as the product of a process of mourning, as the signature of the end of an epoch, or, on the contrary, as an appeal to continue the work that death had interrupted—if not, less charitably, as an appropriation, by which Deleuze, speaking ostensibly of Foucault's thought, in fact promotes his own? When confronted with the question, Deleuze himself invariably evoked a constellation of forces—"out of necessity for me, out of admiration for him, out of the emotion caused by his death and by the interruption of his work," was the succinct response he gave in one interview[2]—but accentuated above all the veritable compulsion (the "necessity for me") that had impelled this gesture of consecrating a text to a "friend philosopher," with this expression to be understood in the sense not only that Deleuze and Foucault were linked by ties of friendship, but, more centrally, that the vital relationship to thought that they shared (as *philo*-sophers, "*friends* of the concept") displayed a particular compatibility, such that the resonance between their respective conceptual creations can be seen to testify to a common image of thought or, in the terms of *What Is Philosophy?*,[3] to an isomorphism of the "plane of immanence" upon which these concepts are deployed. Accordingly, Deleuze emphasized his *Foucault* as stemming from the necessity "to discern the logic of Foucault's thought as a whole" and to delineate thereby a "portrait of Foucault's philosophy" capable of capturing that which, "like a wind that pushes you from behind, in a series of gusts and jolts," would have forced Foucault to pass from one level of his reflection to another, propelling him along a never-pretraced trajectory. This necessity was all the greater, Deleuze added, insofar as he had the impression that this logic—these passages and propulsions—was sorely misunderstood by many readers and commentators.

The comparison of the *Foucault* by Deleuze and the *Deleuze* by Badiou is well-nigh inevitable—if only for the precise reason that the latter, like the former, is a book by an important philosopher on one of his contemporaries. And let us underline this trait: for, despite the paucity of translations of Badiou's work (the only other book so far translated is *Manifesto for Philosophy*, published along with two essays from the collection titled *Conditions*),[4] and the subsequent confidentiality that surrounds his undertaking in English-language countries (a critical commentary, by Jean-Jacques Lecercle, was published in *Radical Philosophy* in early 1999, and an interesting interview in *Artforum*, with Lauren Sedofsky, dates from 1994),[5] Badiou *is* a philosopher of importance. His magnum opus, *L'Etre et l'événement* (Being and event), published in 1988,[6] has been variously hailed (and precisely by Badiou's philosophical peers) as "a book of exceptional scope and rare courage (of thought) that tackles the whole of philosophy, from Parmenides to Heidegger" (Philippe Lacoue-Labarthe); "a significant book...which one cannot fail to find 'staggering,' which one cannot bypass" (Jean-François Lyotard); and "the first book, since *Being and Time*, that again dares to ask the question: 'What of being qua being?' and proffers an answer to it" (Dominique Janicaud).[7] And indeed, something of the scope and audacity of the book may be gauged by the fact that Badiou's answer to "the question of being" entails that ontology must be situated as the concern, not at all of philosophy, but of mathematics, understood as the field of a pure theory of the multiple. In other words, for Badiou, being is the pure multiple (which he names the "inconsistent" multiple, or the multiple "without-one," in stressing thereby the absence of any function of unity), and only a system of thought capable of apprehending pure multiples independently of any characteristic other than their multiplicity is therefore capable of an access to being qua being. The developments within mathematics since Cantor fulfill the requirements that Badiou discerns as those of such a conceptual system: notably, set theory attributes to sets no other essence than that of being a multiplicity, and insofar as this theory further establishes that every set of a set is itself always a set, it is a realization, for Badiou, of the idea that every multiple is the multiple of multiples, without reference to unities of any sort. In positioning set theory less as a particular theory than as the accomplishment of "what can be thought mathematically," Badiou draws the conclusion that it is from its very origin that mathematics has constituted the science of being qua being (although it is only today that we have the means to *know* this), and that philosophy, in clarifying its conditions, must abandon its claim to ontology (although not the identification as such of ontology's belonging to mathematics: *L'Etre et l'événement* examines the axioms of set theory from the point of view of their implications for "classical" philosophical problems involved in the thinking of being) and address itself, on the contrary, to the question of what is *not* being qua being — the question, in other words, of that which exceeds, or in turn "subtracts itself" from, the "subtractive power" of ontology, or mathematics. And here it is important to note that, by "subtractive," Badiou understands (in a sense that is not to be confused with Heidegger's "withdrawal of being") what cannot, in general, be "supposed" by, or in, any form of presence or experience. More specifically, if, for Badiou, being cannot present itself as such (in *a* presentation), it is both because it occurs in *every* "presentation" (the multiple is the very *regime* of presentation) and because, in fact, for something to be presented, a unifying operation, "the count-as-one," must render the multiple consistent; it follows therefore that, from a point of view immanent to the "situation" resulting from this operation (i.e., a situation is defined as a presentation of a *consistent* multiple), the pure multiple, which is absolutely unpresentable in a "count-as-one," is *nothing*; or, in other words, being is what is present in the presentation by way of a subtraction from the count-as-one. Badiou also expresses this by giving to being, or the inconsistency, the name of "void." That admitted, philosophy in addressing the question of what is subtracted from this ontological subtraction becomes "the general theory of the event," for an event is precisely what punctures (or is subtracted from the axioms governing) a situation: it has a "site" in a situation but this does not belong to the latter, it is *supplementary* to it, positioned on the "edge of the void." As a totally chance, incalculable, disconnected supplement that surges forth in a situation and instantly disappears, the event is only recorded in its very disappearance in the form of the linguistic trace that it leaves behind. It is on the basis of these traces that are instigated the *procedures of truth* that it is philosophy's task to seize and organize. In other words, philosophy is not a production of "Truth" but an operation on the basis of the local truths, or procedures of truth, that, relative to a situation, always originate in an event.[8]

Now, given both Badiou's elaboration of an ontology of the multiple, with the attendant conceptualization of the event, and his stature in general (and here, we should add that Badiou is not at all the author of a single book, nor an author confined to a single genre: his philosophical output encompasses some thirteen titles, and he has also written a number of critical and political essays, novels, plays, and even the libretto of an opera, making of him a "complete philosopher" on the Sartrean model), his book on Deleuze—in whose work, of course, the concepts of "multiplicity" and "event" are central—could not fail to arouse an enormous interest in France, both before and upon its publication. This interest was, moreover, all the keener given Badiou's previous, extremely probing discussion of Deleuze's work in an article reviewing *The Fold: Leibniz and the Baroque*,[9] and Deleuze's examination of Badiou's undertaking in a long paragraph of *What Is Philosophy?* (written with Félix Guattari).[10] It was clear that both thinkers centered their respective reflections on the problems of an immanent determination of the multiple, entailing the consequent refusal of all forms of transcendence, and a rigorous theory of the event. Yet, it was no less clear that the ways in which the two thinkers conceived "the multiple" (Badiou) or "multiplicities" (Deleuze) were sharply opposed, with Badiou upholding a "mathematized" paradigm of the multiple, in the tradition of Plato and Descartes, and Deleuze an "organicist" or "vital" paradigm of multiplicities that, if it may be positioned in the tradition of Aristotle and Leibniz, derives most directly from Bergson.[11] For both thinkers, the paradigm adopted by the other proves inadequate to the task of a general theory of multiplicities. For Badiou, Deleuze's organicist doctrine, with its vision of the world/being as a continuous totality and its dependence on the conceptual opposition activity/passivity (or fold/unfold), not only renders it impossible to account for an *event* as the "singularity of a rupture," but reintroduces into a conceptualization of the multiple proclaiming immanence precisely what it seeks to avoid, namely, transcendence; for Deleuze, on the other hand, Badiou's mathematized paradigm of sets condemns his conceptualization of the multiple to remain truncated: he can only succeed in conceiving of numerical, quantitative, extended or "actual" multiplicities, while totally ignoring the conception of qualitative, intensive, "virtual" multiplicities; and yet, for Deleuze, for there to be a "multiplicity" at all, "there must be at least two multiplic*ities*, two types from the outset ... because the multiplicity is precisely what happens between the two."[12] In short, a "philosophical disputation" of a rare tenor had been engaged, and readers were understandably interested in seeing how Badiou would set about explicating the "logic" of Deleuze's thought as a whole. Might not his book present an analysis of Deleuze that proved to be all the finer and the more scrupulous for the fact that, as a philosopher having opted for a different "paradigm," Badiou could feel it all the more necessary to determine rigorously the mechanisms and propulsions that had propelled Deleuze to adopt a vitalist doctrine of multiplicities? Whatever may have been the differing hypotheses or projections fueling the interest in Badiou's book on Deleuze before its publication, however, once the book was published this interest was quickly to find itself transformed—in a way that is strictly comparable, yet again, to the case of Deleuze's *Foucault*—into a reaction of hostile incredulity on the behalf of those whose reading of the text allowed them to discern little or no resemblance in the portrait of the thinker with which they were presented. Indeed, for certain readers, the question of what had compelled Badiou to write his *Deleuze* seemed to have only the most insidious of answers: Badiou, as an "enemy thinker," was set on burying his rival.

And yet, for this very reason, it is perhaps apposite here to remark that Deleuze's evocation of the forces impelling him to write his text on Foucault is not without finding a certain echo in the characterization that Badiou presents in his turn of the forces that led him to publish his *Deleuze*. For although Badiou was, in fact, solicited by the Hachette Publishing Company to write this text for the same series in which he had already written a text on Beckett,[13] his introductory chapter leaves no doubt concerning either the *emotion* that Deleuze's death, and the interruption of his work, occasioned Badiou (who, indeed, narrates throughout these opening pages the sort of love-hate relationship that he maintained with Deleuze from the early 1970s on, until its flowering in the "epistolary controversy"—aptly characterized by one commentator as an "amorous duel"[14]—in which the two men engaged from 1992 to 1994) or the absolute *necessity* that Badiou assigns to the continuation of the philosophical disputation that he and Deleuze had conducted, either directly or indirectly, during the years preceding Deleuze's death. Equally, although Badiou and Deleuze were certainly never "friends" in the existential sense, to the extent that they shared the conviction that philosophy is neither at an end (the "closure of metaphysics"), nor an affair of hermeneutics, or grammatical or logical reductions (and, thus, irreducible to the phenomenological or analytic currents dominant in contemporary philosophy), but must, on the contrary, address itself to the vital task of an "immanent conceptualization of the multiple," the two thinkers may be seen to have formed a "philosophical friendship" of sorts—however opposed they were, in fact, as to the conceptual system that best enables an immanent determination of the multiple. We might then say, in adopting Badiou's own terms, that this was a "conflictual friendship," characterized by the attempt of the two philosopher-protagonists to establish the point at which, despite a certain resonance between their respective conceptual creations, these creations diverge and separate, perhaps attesting thereby to a disparity of the plane on which they are deployed.

It is insofar as Badiou's book on Deleuze ultimately focuses on this divergence that any analogy with Deleuze's *Foucault* undoubtedly best shows its limitations; for at no moment does Deleuze, in his text, play his philosophy off against the philosophy he assigns to Foucault; nor does he ever adopt the point of view of his system to isolate the failures of the other. On the other hand, Badiou engages from the outset a polemical dialogue with Deleuze's conceptualization, in which, if he elaborates—much as Deleuze does in *Foucault*—what he views as the underlying logic and movement of Deleuze's metaphysics, the aim is nevertheless to counter the conceptual coordinates so delineated with arguments that draw on a philosophical tendency opposed to Deleuze's own. As already indicated, however, it is unquestionably the necessity that Badiou assigns to this polemical dialogue as such that compelled him to write this text. And after all, once the central problem that philosophy must deal with today has been defined as the immanent conceptualization of the multiple, it is understandable that a thinker who seeks to elaborate such a conceptualization within the mathematized paradigm of sets, while considering Deleuze to be "the contemporary thinker" of "the other paradigm"—the "vital" paradigm of open multiplicities—should view the continuation and clarification of the disputation between himself and Deleuze concerning this problem as an absolute "necessity": a necessity of the order of thought itself.

That said, the question certainly rests open of whether or not Badiou's book presents—to cite the words that Badiou himself employed when offering a copy to Jean-Clet Martin (equally the author of a text on Deleuze)[15]—a "faithful portrait of the master." But whatever the response to this question (which ultimately each reader must decide for himself or herself), there is no doubting the fact that Badiou, in delineating this portrait, was animated by an iconoclastic intention to shatter the existing images of Deleuze. Up to now, if we are to believe Badiou, there has been nothing but *misrepresentations* of Deleuze's philosophy—including, perhaps, a certain image harbored or promulgated by Deleuze himself.

What Badiou names the "superficial doxa of an anarcho-desiring Deleuzianism," making of Deleuze the champion of desire, free flux, and anarchic experimentation, is the first of the false images he sets out to shatter. And here, English-language readers, whose reception of Deleuze has been filtered through the achronology of translations and the emphasis of commentators on the playful and extravagant aspects of Deleuze's collaboration with Félix Guattari, most notably in *Anti-Oedipus*, will bear the full brunt of Badiou's scathing dismissal of the gross inadequacy of such a representation; for although Badiou attacks specifically the "an-archizing ideal of the sovereign individual populating the Earth with the productions of his/her desire," denouncing this reading as the substitution of a consumerist sat-isfaction of desires to a sober doctrine advocating an ascetic and impersonal ethics of thought, his critique of the doxa surrounding Deleuze encompasses no less deci-sively the depiction that is (still) often proffered by English-language readers of Deleuze as refusing all systematicity, as resolutely breaking with "the metaphysical tradition,"[16] and as completely unconcerned by questions of such a "classical" ilk as those, for example, of transcendental conditions or ontology.

Contrary to such received ideas, Badiou affirms Deleuze to pro-pose a metaphysics (which, in fact, concurs with Deleuze's own repeated claim that he felt himself to be "a pure metaphysicist")[17] and one of the great merits of his book undoubtedly lies in its insistence that a comprehension of Deleuze's work must necessarily address the question of the complex nature of the metaphysical system elaborated therein. "One misses everything if one disregards such explicit declara-tions as: 'philosophy merges with ontology' or 'from Parmenides to Heidegger...a single voice raises the clamor of being.'" In this perspective, Badiou underlines above all the importance for Deleuze of the thesis of the univocity of being, in which the essential — according to a passage of *Difference and Repetition* that Badiou reproduces in the selection of texts at the end of his essay — is that "Being is said in a single and same sense of all its individuating differences or intrinsic modalities.... Being is said in a single and same sense of everything of which it is said, but that of which it is said differs: it is said of difference itself." In situating this thesis at the very core of Deleuze's thought, Badiou remarks, moreover, that his book as a whole is pre-cisely an attempt to elucidate what is to be understood by this decisive univocity — the point here being, of course, that such an elucidation is both necessary and diffi-cult because the full implications of this thesis for Deleuze's thought have as yet remained ungrasped. And indeed, it is at this juncture that Badiou situates the second of the images of Deleuze that must be shattered: for all those who believe Deleuze to have constructed what might be termed a "transcendental-immanent" metaphysics that inseparably links the univocity of being to the movement of singularities or multiplicities, in situating "the multiple" as constitutive of the virtual "univocal" plane of immanence (along the lines of the equation, noted by Deleuze in one of his letters to Badiou, "immanence = univocity"),[18] or, more simply, all those who believe Deleuze to be first and foremost a thinker of multiplicities (along the lines of the formula, in *A Thousand Plateaus*, "monism = pluralism") are, in Badiou's eyes, suffer-ing from an illusion, no less than those who subscribe to the anarcho-desiring ideal.

The truth of the matter, according to Badiou, is that Deleuze's fundamental concern, in upholding ontological univocity, is not the "liberation of the multiple" but the formulation of a "renewed concept of the One," in terms of which the multiple is conceived as the immanent production of this One. This, in fact, means that the multiple has a purely formal or modal, and not *real*, status (for the multiple attests the power of the One, in which consists its ontological status) and is thus, ultimately, of the order of simulacra. Deleuze, moreover, fully assumes this consequence of the thesis of univocity, if we are to believe Badiou's portrait, when he affirms "the rights of the simulacrum" against Platonism's hierarchy of being in which simulacra are devalued as degraded copies, unequal to some supposed model or real archetype. That being the case, however, Deleuzianism is positioned as fundamentally a "Platonism with a different accentuation": rejecting the mimetic vision of being (which poses beings as copies of a form of Being) and the accompanying determination of the "ground" in terms of an ideal Model founding the play of appearances, Deleuze nonetheless "retains from Plato the univocal sovereignty of the One" and upholds that "beings are of the order of simulacra," while "rethinking," at the same time, the notion of ground as a virtual totality expressing the eternal truth of temporal actualization. In short, Deleuze's inflexible upholding of the thesis of univocity is at the price of elaborating, *despite himself* (Deleuze is qualified by Badiou as an "involuntary Platonist"), a system of thought whose final identity is that of a "Platonism of the virtual."

The image of Deleuzianism as a thought affirming multiplicities as an order of difference that cannot be subjugated to the Identical, to the One, is not simply demolished by Badiou, but literally erased. In the face of such iconoclastic zeal, which overrides even "the apparent indications of the work," it is hard not to think of the "violence" with which Heidegger conducted what he himself (ultimately) termed his "overinterpretation" of Kant—with the justification, in the case of such an "overinterpretation," being, of course, that the logic of a system of thought is not necessarily apparent to its author. Yet interestingly, although Badiou's interpretation of Deleuze does indeed seem to subscribe to Heidegger's characterization of an authentic philosophical "laying out" (*Auslegung*) of a work as necessarily having to use violence in order to bring out "the unsaid" that the author "had wanted to say,"[19] it is precisely *against* what this interpretation discerns as the logic of Deleuze's thought—what Deleuze "had wanted to say"—that Badiou delivers his most violent blows.

Badiou's portrait of Deleuzianism as a metaphysics of the One (or One-All), concerned above all with upholding the univocity of being and with instating the virtual (identified as the dynamic agency of the One) as the "ground" for the actual (as simulacrum), is finally a portrait of a philosophical project doomed to failure in its own terms; for the very method of proceeding by pairs of concepts—such as the virtual and the actual, chance and the eternal return, or the fold and the Outside—which this project deploys in order to intuit the movement of the One itself and thus attain the univocity of being, proves, in Badiou's analyses, to reintroduce an equivocity of sense, despite all Deleuze's attempts to the contrary. Badiou targets specifically the conceptual couple of the virtual and the actual, claiming that, insofar as the virtual functions as the "ground" of the actual, a problem ensues for Deleuze's determination of entities as being split into a virtual part and an actual part—a virtual and an actual "image"—which cannot, however, be thought of as explicitly separate or distinguishable from each other, for any real separation runs counter to univocity. On the one hand, the optical metaphor (the parts as images) does not hold up, according to Badiou, and thus, this doctrine concerning the object's parts cannot avoid falling into equivocity, whereby Being is said according to the division of the actual and the virtual: Badiou, in fact, views Deleuze's category of the virtual as maintaining a transcendence that is transposed "beneath" the actual beings or simulacra of the world. On the other hand, even were this doctrine effectively to avoid equivocity by rendering the two parts indiscernible, the virtual would, in this case, no longer fulfill its role as a ground of the actual (for the indiscernibility would render that for which it serves as ground essentially indeterminable). Deleuze's procedure founders therefore under its own presuppositions, with equivocity being reinstalled at the heart of being itself and with the virtual finally having the status of a "final cause" that explains everything only to the extent that it explains nothing at all.

Clearly, the arguments of Badiou's book are not only provocative, but also highly controversial. As already mentioned, since its publication in France, dissenting voices have indeed raised a certain "clamor," with Badiou's portrait being denounced as the "false" and "shocking" reduction of Deleuze's thought of fluid and molecular multiplicities that escape classical philosophical grids (such as, precisely, the opposition between the One and the multiple) to the ultraclassical problematic of a hypostasized One and representation (or truth). On the numerous occasions when Badiou has affronted his critics publicly, he has rarely failed to address each objection raised against his book, point by point (Badiou's style of verbal presentation is no less systematic and "affirmative"—he usually proceeds by series of theses and definitions—than that of his written work), in reaffirming and often reinforcing both the broad lines and the detailed analyses that compose his portrait of Deleuze. As a general statement of the principles governing his philosophical drafts-manship, we might note here his response to the basic criticism that the Deleuze who emerges from his presentation is quite simply unrecognizable. Reiterating first the reasons why he himself believes his book to present less an "unrecognizable" than an "uncomfortable," or, one might say, "nonconformist," portrait of Deleuze, Badiou, in answering this objection, went on to state that his reading of Deleuze can be seen to operate on exactly the same lines as Deleuze's own reading of other philosophers: one "approaches the author from behind" and forces the latter to give birth to a philosophical "offspring" that is indeed his, although singularly different from the "official" progeny (or the family resemblance, one might say) to which the author's proper name has been conferred.[20] This evocation of Deleuze's own opera-tion of forcing others to bring forth "monstrous," unexpected, philosophical offspring aptly underlines the fact that the history of philosophy is a history of successive ap-propriations, which can take the form of malevolent mistreatments or violent per-versions, of timorous transmissions, vapid incomprehension, or uninspired repro-duction, of congenial encounters, revigorating regeneration, or marriages of true minds. And in this sense, whether one is ultimately persuaded by Badiou's portrait of Deleuze, which, of a consistently philosophical tenor, is expressed in a precise and always "assured" prose, or whether one reacts allergically to a "montage" making of Deleuze a misshapen, "unrecognizable" creature, one is forcefully incited—for this, too, is the lesson that should be drawn from the history of philosophy—to a rereading and rethinking (be this by way of reevaluation or reaffirmation) of Deleuze's corpus as a whole. Moreover, one might, for this reason alone, describe *Deleuze: The Clamor of Being* as presenting its readers with a formidable exercise in philosophical discipline: the fact that Badiou's reading is unquestionably controversial but under-lines the extreme tension characterizing the discernment of what questions are to be asked in philosophy and of philosophy.

Although translation is always a painstaking affair, in which—unlike, perhaps, philo-sophical interpretations—fidelity does not have the leeway to branch off into non-resemblance, in the case of a book such as Badiou's, which stages a "philosophical disputation" drawing on two distinct philosophical systems, the translator is obvi-ously forced to redouble her or his attention to terminological consistency and to the exact rendering of conceptual "deployments" (by which I mean the—often ex-tremely intricate—relations established between elements of a concept or between one concept and another). Badiou may well write a French that is as classical in syn-tax as it is in measure (as is to be expected from an author whose writing for the theater has been characterized as "Claudelian"), he may well employ a predominantly short, concise sentence and paragraph structure in this book, he is no less capable of taking hold of a concept and sinuously enfolding it within a proliferation of relations in such a way that, under an ordered procession of implications that seems governed by concerns of methodical precision alone, he in fact effects a subtle inflection and reordering of the elements encompassed by the concept in question. This being the case, I have attempted to keep the translation as close as possible to the original structure of Badiou's sentences, in order to respect the order and relations between both the elements and the "concatenations" (to employ a word to which we shall return) of Badiou's conceptual machinery.

The task of respecting terminological consistency was all the more important given that Deleuze's many books have been translated into English by almost as many different hands. Thus, I have often modified the existing translations of the passages that Badiou cites in his text and the extracts from Deleuze's work presented in the Appendix simply in order to ensure that a concept used by Deleuze is, at all times and in all contexts, rendered by the one and same English word. For example, the term *singularité*—in which we can recognize one of Deleuze's major concepts—has been rendered as "particular feature" in the translation of Deleuze's *Foucault*, but is more commonly translated by its English cognate "singularity" (as in *Difference and Repetition* and *The Logic of Sense*,[21] among other places); accordingly, I have chosen the latter term as the translation of all occurrences of the word *singularité* in Badiou's text, including the quoted passages from *Foucault*. Another example of this type concerns the different renderings of *renverser* (as frequently found in the expression *renverser le Platonisme*): translated as "to reverse" in *The Logic of Sense*, this term is rendered as "to overturn" in *Difference and Repetition*. I have preferred to use consistently the latter rendering here, insofar as it seems to me to have the advantage both of conforming to the translation of the German *Umdrehen* adopted in the English translation of Heidegger's book *Nietzsche*[22]—which is, of course, in many ways the "source" of the expression "the overturning of Platonism"—and, at the same time, of not "prejudicing" the manner in which this Nietzschean program is to be understood (as might "reversal," with its implication of a simple inversion of a dichotomous structure that leaves the structure as such untouched: of course, Heidegger finally upheld this interpretation, whereas Deleuze, on the contrary, explicitly distinguished his use of the expression from any such understanding of Nietzsche's undertaking).

Slightly different considerations underlie the consistent translation of the word *multiple* by its English cognate. The importance of the two concepts *le multiple* and *multiplicités* in the disputation between Badiou and Deleuze (with Badiou claiming that Deleuze fails to uphold an immanent conceptualization of the "multiple," Deleuze that Badiou remains at the level of *one* type of "multiplicity" alone) rendered it necessary from the outset that the resonance between the two terms be respected: indeed, Badiou plays very subtly on this similarity, as a means of realigning, one might say, Deleuze's problematic of multiplicities with the classical problem opposing the One to the multiple. And although an English-language philosopher would more naturally express this latter opposition as that between "the One and the Many," the fact that the term "multiplicity" is now well established in the translations of Deleuze's work disqualified the choice of rendering *multiple* by "many" and *multiplicité* by "manifold," and enforced that the English word "multiple" be retained as the translation for *multiple* in all its occurrences—including those where "many" would, indeed, be the more appropriate term. That said, readers should remember that Deleuze constantly relates Bergson's use of the term *multiplicité* (from which his own acceptation of this term derives) to the mathematical theory of Georg Riemann, who, by his distinction between discreet "multiplicities" and continuous "multiplicities," established the definition of what mathematicians precisely refer to (in English) as Riemannian "manifolds."

The translation of the word *fond* (derived from the Latin *fundus*: "bottom" and "piece of land"), as well as the associated series of cognate terms—*fonder, fondation, le sans fond,* and especially *fondement*—which Badiou plays on in the decisive fourth chapter of his book dealing with Deleuze's notion of the virtual, posed particular problems. The important use that Deleuze makes of these terms in both *Difference and Repetition* and *The Logic of Sense* displays a crucial distinction between *fond* and *fondement.* Succinctly put, this is a distinction between a nonmediated formless "bottom"—that, if it is a "ground" in the sense of the underlying reality or basis of "what is," is one that lies behind every other "ground" capable of explaining or affording a sufficient reason for the "world" as it appears, and that, for this reason, may be said to be differentiated from *le sans fond* or "the groundless" less in terms of its "nature" than by the relations that it enters into or that are established between its components—and the "foundation" or "ground" that precisely results from "the operation of logos, or of sufficient reason" and serves as the underpinning for the forms of representation. Obviously, given such a distinction, it would be preferable to translate the two French cognates by different English words. And, of course, having integrated both Latin and German roots, the English language does offer us two series of cognates by which to translate the series of cognates of *fond:* for, the English "found" is cognate with the Latin *fundus*, while "ground" is cognate with the German *Grund* (both deriving from the Germanic *grunduz). One might thus be tempted to translate *fondement* by "foundation" (rendering *fondation* by "act—or operation—of founding"), and retain "ground" for *fond*. The problem with this solution, however, is that the standard philosophical translation of *fondement* is, precisely, "ground" (with both the French and the English word, of course, translating the German *Grund*). Moreover, it is significative that, of the two terms *fondement* and *fond*, only *fondement* (with, of course, the cognate *fonder*) figures in the time-honored (and French Academy–sanctioned) Lalande vocabulary of philosophical terms,[23] while *fond* is classified, in the more recent *Dictionary of Philosophical Notions*,[24] as an aesthetic notion ("background"), in contrast to *fondement*, listed as belonging to general philosophy. Given additionally that Badiou uses indifferently *fond* or *fondement* in the sense of the traditional philosophical notion of "ground" or "foundation," there thus seemed little option other than to translate both French words by "ground" (which is also the choice of Paul Patton, in his translation of *Difference and Repetition*), although, given the importance of their distinction in Deleuze's thought, I have included the French in the text wherever "ground" translates *fond* and not *fondement*.[25] That said, the importance of this distinction for Badiou's text may seem minimal. As mentioned, Badiou's own use of the terms *fondement* and *fond* does not, contrary to Deleuze's use of these terms, mark any conceptual differentiation. Hence, one might claim that there is no need for readers familiar with *Difference and Repetition* or *The Logic of Sense* to be able to recognize the term that Badiou employs as corresponding to a specific term employed by Deleuze (which, in the case of *Difference and Repetition*, they would be unable to do anyway, insofar as both *fond* and *fondement* have been translated in this text as "ground," without any way of knowing which French word is involved). And yet, to put it very succinctly, the fact that Badiou does not "recognize" Deleuze's distinction is absolutely central to the interpretation that he proposes of Deleuze's philosophy; it is, to paraphrase Badiou himself, an issue that lies at the very heart of his and Deleuze's controversy. For this reason, it did indeed seem necessary that readers be able to discern the specific French word translated by "ground."

An inverse case to the above (where it was a matter of translating two distinct French words by one and the same English word) is the translation of the word *tout*, when used as a simple substantive *le Tout* or as found in the locution *Un-Tout*, by two distinct English words, namely: "all" and "whole." This dual rendering of *tout*—my sole exception to the rule of consistency—amounts, in fact, to retaining alongside one another the different translations of this term that figure, most notably, in the English-language editions of *Difference and Repetition* and *Cinema 1:*

The Movement-Image.[26] Thus, in referring to the selection of texts at the end of Badiou's text, one finds, in the first extract from *Difference and Repetition*, Deleuze's description of "nomadic" distribution as involving "things being divided up within being in the univocity of simple presence (the One-All) [*l'Un-Tout*]," whereas, in the extract from the first volume on the cinema, one finds Bergson's third thesis on movement said to entail that "movement is a mobile section of duration, that is, of the Whole, or of a whole [*du Tout, ou d'un tout*]." As the English translations of Bergson's texts do indeed use "whole" to render *tout*, I judged the use of "all" in contexts where Deleuze is referring to Bergson (or Badiou is referring to Deleuze referring to Bergson) as inappropriate; on the other hand, "One-All" is a consecrated locution within classical texts (above all, in the Neoplatonist tradition, although one might also cite in this instance the exclamation attributed to Xenophanes: "The All is One")[27] and thus, indeed, the appropriate rendering for a concept dealing with the univocity of being. Interestingly, these two acceptations are brought together to a certain extent by Deleuze himself, in his book *Bergsonism*, in the context of his discussion of Bergson's monism as entailing the coexistence of all the degrees of difference (from matter to duration) in one Time, which is nature itself. Insisting on the fact that this coexistence of all the degrees (Bergson's "whole") is virtual, Deleuze effectively goes on to remark that this virtual "point of unification" is "not without resembling the One-All [*Un-Tout*] of the Platonists" (or, more precisely, of the Neoplatonists).[28] That said, Deleuze's comparison of Bergson's "whole" and the Neoplatonist "One-All" does not, in itself, entail that his own acceptation is conform to a Neoplatonism encompassing the procession and hypostases of being.

The only significant instance in which I have preferred to introduce a new translation of one of Deleuze's terms, rather than abide by established renderings (in choosing eventually between different existing translations when necessary for terminological coherency), is my translation of *ré-enchaînement* (which is encountered especially in the expression *ré-enchaînement perpetuel*) by "reconcatenation," rather than "relinking." As Alain Badiou writes in his third chapter, when he develops his own particular interpretation of what Deleuze means by this term, *ré-enchaînement* is an expression that Deleuze frequently employs—and even in those of Deleuze's books where the term is not explicitly used, the underlying concept is no less strongly present. Deleuze's use of the expression derives (via Raymond Ruyer) from the work of the Russian mathematician Andrei Markov, who established a type of relation (precisely named a Markov chain or process) that concerns semifortuitous phenomena or mixtures of dependency and uncertainty, distinguished from both determined concatenations and chance distributions.[29] What Deleuze essentially wishes to indicate by this expression is, in my mind, the operation of reserializing a series (somewhat in the way that Kant's synthesis of reproduction is the synthesizing or serialization of a succession): for this reason, the word "concatenation," defined as "the linking together in a series or chain," seems to me to capture more appropriately than does the less accentuated "linking" the underlying reference both to Markov chains and to the concept of series that runs through Deleuze's entire work. Of course, given the importance of the *re*doing or repetition of such a concatenation in Deleuze's thought (it figures nothing less than the power proper to difference as such), it was absolutely imperative to modify those instances in existing translations of Deleuze's work where *ré-enchaînement* has been rendered by "linking" alone.

One final remark concerning the translation of terms specific to Deleuze's conceptual vocabulary needs to be made. Readers familiar with *Difference and Repetition* will recall that this text extensively employs a terminological distinction between "to differen*t*iate" and "to differen*c*iate," with this latter term being a neologism introduced by the translator, Paul Patton, in order to respect the distinction between the two French words *différentier* and *différencier*. The habitual meaning of the first of these French words is restricted to the mathematical operation consisting in the calculation of derivatives, whereas the second refers to the operation of making different or of constituting the difference between entities in the wide sense covered by the English verb "to differentiate" (whose semantic range also encompasses, of course, the technical, mathematical, meaning). In his adoption of this distinction, Deleuze uses the mathematical term to refer to the operation of difference in its virtual aspect, whereas *différencier*, or *différenciation*, is synonymous with the process of actualization, and accordingly Patton, in following this distinction, restricts "to differentiate" and "differentiation" to the virtual operation and coins "to differenciate" and "differenciation" to cover the operation of actualization. This being the case, readers will encounter this terminological distinction in certain passages cited by Badiou in his text, as well as in the second of the extracts from *Difference and Repetition* reproduced in the Appendix. However, all other occurrences of "to differentiate" or "differentiation" encountered in Badiou's text must be understood to be "unmarked" occurrences: that is, Badiou's use of the term *différencier* does not adhere to the opposition *différentier/différencier*, and hence he uses this term in contexts dealing with the immanent deployment of the virtual where, were the terminological distinction made in *Difference and Repetition* respected, one would expect to find the verb *différentier*. Inversely, I have never used the neologism "to differenciate" in the translation.

Badiou's own terminology poses fewer problems of translation, and when such problems have occurred, in instances that almost all concern the Heideggerian reference or resonance of a specific term employed by Badiou, I have included translator's notes that are given at the end of the volume. On the other hand, however, there are occasions on which his terminology may well pose problems of comprehension for the reader insofar as it refers to the conceptual apparatus developed in *L'Etre et l'événement*: accordingly, I have equally inserted explicatory notes whenever this seemed necessary to facilitate the understanding of the text. In this context, I would, moreover, signal that, in fact, all the notes found in the text (with the obvious exception of the Appendix, in which the notes are Deleuze's, other than the one or two instances where I have adjoined a translator's note) are mine: Badiou is an author who is habitually parsimonious with notes, with many of his texts, like this one, doing without altogether, while in *L'Etre et l'événement* he adopts a system of including a limited number of notes that are completely "facultative," in the sense that no index is given in the text itself and readers are simply informed that, if they feel the need to know more on a certain point, they can turn to the end of the book to see if Badiou furnishes further details.

The last remark that needs to be made concerns punctuation: in particular the capitalization or not of the word "being." I have scrupulously respected Badiou's use of capitalization and lowercase throughout the text, and hence have only capitalized the word "being" where *être* is capitalized in the original text. Readers should be forewarned that there is in Badiou's discourse a certain confluence of Heidegger's thought of ontological difference, instating being (or "Being" with a capital letter) as distinct or as differing from beings or entities—and no longer, as in metaphysics, the ground of beings—and his own acceptation of being as the being of beings (with the "of" marking a subjective complement: being as the "essence" of beings). Until recently, most English and French translations of Heidegger opted for the capitalization of "Being" (or *Etre*),[30] and Badiou's own use of uppercase and lowercase seems to follow more or less this procedure when he refers to "Being" in the sense, one might say, of "the fold of being and beings," or the "object" of ontology (in a sense wide enough to encompass Heidegger's inflection, but stopping short of Badiou's own attribution of ontology to mathematics); but this is not a hard-and-fast rule. Readers will encounter the expression "the being of beings" cast entirely in lowercase letters in a context referring explicitly to Heidegger's asking the question of Being, but they will equally encounter the same expression with the capitalization of the first "b" ("the Being of beings"). Similarly, they will encounter dense passages where it is a question of the "being of the simulacrum and the simulacrum of Being," or of the virtual as, at once, "the being of the actual," "the being of virtualities," and "the very Being of beings." None of this is necessarily confusing, but readers do need to be attentive—especially given that the word "being" is also the translation of *étant*, although in this case I have consistently used the plural "beings" wherever possible (and Badiou does usually employ the plural *étants* rather than the singular *l'étant*), whereas in all instances where it was necessary to respect the singular form, I have used an indefinite article or a particularizing adjective ("a being," or "a singular being") to avoid any confusion. That said, there is one occurrence in the text where the expression "a being" translates *un être* and not *un étant*, but the context (Badiou speaks in this instance of "a being of the simulacrum" [p. 36]) should prevent any misunderstanding. Finally, considerations of consistency in this respect led me to modify a number of quotations from Deleuze's texts (especially *The Logic of Sense*), predominantly by replacing "Being" with the lowercase "being" in all instances where Deleuze himself writes *être* rather than *Etre*.

Translation, I have already stated, is a painstaking affair. My thanks are due to a number of people who unsparingly gave of their time and expertise in the course of preparing this translation. Alain Badiou was extremely supportive from the very outset and kindly answered my successive queries throughout the process. Jean-Pierre Tillos patiently explained numerous nuances of the French text, and Jennifer McCamley and Richard Lynch proofread the entire manuscript of the translation: the text as it stands owes much to their labor. Christophe Campos, Susan Davies, Jean-Pierre Leininger, Brian Massumi, and Eon Yorck gave assistance on particular points. I would also like to thank François Cusset, of the French Publisher's Agency, for his support at the inception of this project, and William Murphy, my editor at the University of Minnesota Press, for his patience throughout it.

Works by Gilles Deleuze

THROUGHOUT THIS book, the author cites Gilles Deleuze's works and incorporates these references into the text. Extracts from Deleuze's writings are also included in the Appendix. The page references given in the text correspond to the following English translations:

Difference and Repetition, translated by Paul Patton (New York: Columbia University Press, 1994).

Foucault, translated by Seán Hand (Minneapolis: University of Minnesota Press, 1988).

The Fold: Leibniz and the Baroque, translated by Tom Conley (Minneapolis: University of Minnesota Press, 1993).

The Logic of Sense, translated by Mark Lester with Charles Stivale (New York: Columbia University Press, 1990).

Cinema 1: The Movement-Image, translated by Hugh Tomlinson and Barbara Habberjam (Minneapolis: University of Minnesota Press, 1986).

Cinema 2: The Time-Image, translated by Hugh Tomlinson and Robert Galeta (Minneapolis: University of Minnesota Press, 1989).

So Near! So Far!

WHAT A strange story my nonrelationship with Gilles Deleuze makes.

He was older than I for reasons other than age. When I was a student at the Ecole normale supérieure[1] forty years ago, we were already aware that we could hear extraordinary lectures at the Sorbonne, which, ranging from Hume to *La Nouvelle Héloïse*, were singularly different from everything that was recited elsewhere. Deleuze's lectures. I got people to pass me their notes, to recount the tone, the style, as well as the astonishing corporeal presence that bore the invention of concepts. But — even then — I did not attend, I did not see him.

In the early sixties, I read him, without as yet finding in his thought either a major support or an identifiable adversary for the explorations that I was tentatively making between my Sartrean adolescence and my frequentation of Althusser, Lacan, and mathematical logic. It was more singular, more arresting, than useful for my meanderings. His canonical references (the Stoics, Hume, Nietzsche, Bergson...) were the opposite of my own (Plato, Hegel, Husserl). Even when it came to mathematics — which, I recognized, keenly interested him — Deleuze's preferences were for differential calculus and Riemannian manifolds, from which he drew powerful metaphors (and yes, I do mean metaphors). I preferred algebra and sets. Spinoza was a point of intersection but "his" Spinoza was (and still is) for me an unrecognizable creature.

Then came the red years, 1968, the University of Vincennes.[2] For the Maoist that I was, Deleuze, as the philosophical inspiration for what we called the "anarcho-desirers," was an enemy all the more formidable for being internal to the "movement" and for the fact that his course was one of the focal points of the university. I have never tempered my polemics: *consensus* is not one of my strong points. I attacked him with the heavy verbal artillery of the epoch. Once, I even commanded a "brigade" of intervention in his course. I wrote, under the characteristic title "Flux and the Party," an enraged article against his conceptions (or supposed conceptions) of the relationship between politics and mass movements. Deleuze remained impassive, almost paternal. He spoke of me as an "intellectual suicide."

He only really got angry, as did Jean-François Lyotard, when, beginning with an obscure affair concerning the status of nontenured lecturers, he had the impression that, flanked by François Regnault and Jean Borreil,[3] I was attempting to take over the running of the department for political ends. He signed a text in which I was accused of wanting the "Bolshevization" of the department— which was either extremely flattering in my regard or, more probably, indicative of an extremely narrow idea of the Bolsheviks! Following which, the legitimate troika, Deleuze-Châtelet-Lyotard, retook "power" without resistance.

Faithful to Nietzsche, Deleuze was not, in his thinking, a man of *ressentiment*. Every text must be read as a beginning, and not according to self-interested reckonings of its present utility or retrospective returns. I learned that he had spoken approvingly of my little book *De l'idéologie*[4] for the way in which I put into play, at the core of political processes, the distinction between "class" and "mass." And this at almost the very moment—it was the period of the decomposition of "leftist" forces, when, given my never renounced fidelity to this political tendency, I was irked by any visible flagging—that I tended rather to identify as "fascist" his apologia for the spontaneous movement, his theory of "spaces of liberty," his hatred for the dialectic: in sum, his philosophy of life and the natural One-All.

"Bolshevik" versus "fascist": what a fine pair we made!

However, almost immediately afterwards, I was struck by his vigorous public intervention against the "New Philosophers," who, in claiming to modify the relation of freely imposed reserve that philosophers have traditionally adopted toward opinion and the media, and in acting as spokesmen for the "vulgar critique" of communism, were accurately perceived by Deleuze as constituting a menace for thought itself.[5] I started to say to myself that, when a new period is opened and other adversaries climb onto the stage, conceptual alliances shift or are overturned.

In 1982, I published a philosophical book of transition, *Théorie du sujet*,[6] in which I attempted to refound the dialectic in a framework compatible with the political givens of the time as well as with my Mallarméan and mathematical studies. Deleuze sent me a small favorable note, which, given the public isolation in which I found myself (the period was that of the rallying to the left, to Mitterrandism, that I abhorred) and the supremely contemptuous silence about what I was trying to do in philosophy that went with this, touched me greatly. The least that one can say is that he was under no obligation to make such a gesture. And all the more so given that he himself had agreed to have lunch with the president, which I found completely scandalous. How he must have laughed!

Note that, with the exception of extremely rare institutional occasions (I boycotted practically all university and departmental events, other than my courses), I had still not, in 1982, "met" Deleuze. I had never had dinner with him, or gone to his home; nor had we ever had a drink together, or exchanged words during a stroll. Nor, alas, was this to ever happen afterwards, in the period before his death.

As in billiards, the "moves" of intersubjectivity are often indirect. The change of epoch—in philosophy—was signaled to me by a long theoretical discussion with Jean-François Lyotard that took place in his car on the way back from a meeting at the home of Châtelet, who was already very ill. Lyotard was later to compare this pacified episode to a meeting "under the tent" of two protagonists who had been mortal enemies the day before. Not long afterwards, Lyotard proposed to me that I review what he called his "philosophy book." The text in question was *The Differend*.[7] I accepted without hesitation; the article, published in *Critique*, substituted analysis, comparison, and objection for the simple summary of political antagonisms.[8] Let us say that the invectives ("Bolshevik!" "Fascist!"), expressing the vitality of movements, gave way to the reflective determination of intellectual incompatibilities (philosophy of the event of truth against postmodern philosophy), which, under the frozen surface of Mitterrandian consensus, expressed the latent force of thoughts to come.

The publication of *L'Etre et l'événement*, in 1988, sealed—for me—the definitive entry into this new period.[9] I gradually became aware that, in developing an ontology of the multiple, it was vis-à-vis Deleuze and no one else that I was positioning my endeavor. For there are two paradigms that govern the manner in which the multiple is thought, as Deleuze's texts indicate from very early on: the "vital" (or "animal") paradigm of open multiplicities (in the Bergsonian filiation) and the mathematized paradigm of sets, which can also be qualified as "stellar" in Mallarmé's sense of the word. That being the case, it is not too inexact to maintain that Deleuze is the contemporary thinker of the first paradigm, and that I strive to harbor the second, including its most extreme consequences. Moreover, the notion of "multiplicity" was to be at the center of our epistolary controversy of 1992–94, with him maintaining that I confuse "multiple" and "number," whereas I maintained that it is inconsistent to uphold, in the manner of the Stoics, the virtual Totality or what Deleuze named "chaosmos," because, with regard to sets, there can be neither a universal set, nor All, nor One.

That it was not absurd to compare the two of us was gradually to become a public conviction. In 1992, François Wahl based the organization of the preface that he kindly wrote for the collection of my texts, published under the title *Conditions*, on the doublet Badiou/Deleuze.[10] Later, Éric Alliez, in his "report" on contemporary French philosophy written from a Deleuzian perspective, was, however, to position my efforts as forming part of the move "out of" phenomenology that, in his eyes, was brought to completion by his master.[11]

The question, certainly, is neither one of identity, nor even of convergence. Rather, it concerns a direct opposition that can, however, be conceptually assigned to a shared conviction as to what it is possible to demand of philosophy today and the central problem that it must deal with: namely, an *immanent* conceptualization of the multiple.

When, in 1989, during the brief endeavor to modify the state of philosophical criticism that was represented by *Annuaire philosophique*, the question of a text on *The Fold* came up, it was with real satisfaction that I volunteered.[12] I was impressed and fascinated by the book. To my mind, I did full justice to the text, without compromising in any way. Some people, with long memories, were to maintain that, after having politically insulted Deleuze fifteen years previously, I had no "right"—without an intermediary self-criticism—to acclaim him as I did. This was in no way my opinion. Political sequences, bearing the stamp of the event, are one thing; philosophical eternity, even if, in its construction, it is conditioned by politics, is another. Nor was it, so it seemed, Deleuze's opinion: after reading my text, he sent me an attentive and extremely friendly, almost tender, letter. He concluded that the only thing for him to do in the circumstances was to take a stance, in his turn, concerning my concepts. With this remark, I became finally convinced that we constituted, without ever having decided to do so (on the contrary!), a sort of paradoxical tandem.

A period of truly sustained theoretical discussion began in 1991. I was responsible for initiating it and, for me, it was the result of the sudden coming together of three elements:

- The fact that Gilles Deleuze had been working for many years with Félix Guattari in a context of convergence and quasi fusion. Might he not be open to a "collaboration" that was, this time, divergent or contrasting? After all, in his theory of series, priority is systematically given to divergence, while convergence is considered to be only a "closed" case of actualization.

- The conviction that "together" we could at least highlight our total and positive serenity, our active indifference, concerning the omnipresent theme of "the end of philosophy."

- The idea of reviving the great classical controversies, that were neither closed, self-engrossed altercations nor petty "debates," but rather, forceful oppositions seeking to cut straight to the *sensitive point* at which different conceptual creations separate.

Accordingly, I proposed to Deleuze that we correspond for as long as would be necessary to establish our mobile divergence in its exact confused clarity (or obscure distinctness). He replied that this idea suited him.

At that time, he was terminating a decisive (convergent) collaboration with Félix Guattari, *What Is Philosophy?*;[13] the book was to have an enormous and legitimate success. One finds here the note on me that Deleuze had announced he would write after my article on *The Fold*. In reply, and in order to prepare the terrain, I devoted four of my seminars at the Collège international de philosophie to the best-seller of Deleuze and Guattari, without understating their position (I really went into the details), but without toning down my criticisms either.[14]

It seemed to me at this moment that Deleuze was hesitating about putting our epistolary protocol into effect. I well understood that there were great pools of darkness that contributed to this hesitation, which had been building up over a long time: Guattari's death, for example, which was like a mutilation, and his own increasingly precarious health, which made the very act of writing a sort of exploit, violently wrested from an adversary several hours a day. One has to have received, as I did, those long slanted, slashed letters that were trembling and determined at the same time, to be able to understand the very painful and fugitive victory that writing—thinking—can be. And then, however free he might have been of the stigmata of the past, however oriented, both doctrinally and vitally, toward creative affirmation and new experiences, there was no doubt that Deleuze had all the best reasons in the world not to associate his immense philosophical prestige with the elaboration, however contrasting it may be, of my own pursuit. Why should he be of service to me, who had so violently vilified him, me from whom everything separated him, even if in our case we had succeeded in attaining calm, and even fraternal, shores after our controversy?

Confirming my fears, he ended up writing to me that, most decidedly, he did not have time, in view of his precarious health, to engage in the correspondence. He would content himself with one detailed letter of evaluation and questions. I received this admirable letter and replied to it, attempting to prove myself equal to the situation. He replied to my response, and so on it went: the impossibility unfolded, making real what had been declared impossible. Dozens of pages piled up.

In late 1994, we decided that we had completed the task, that we would not go any further. For both of us, the work of clarification had been effected. Shortly afterwards, Deleuze wrote me that, after having reread his letters, he found them too "abstract," not up to the occasion. He announced, rather abruptly, that he had destroyed the copies of his letters and indicated unambiguously that he would oppose, if ever anyone should have the idea, any form of circulation, not to mention publication, of these texts.

At the time, viewing this final assessment as a sort of disavowal of our exchanges, I was somewhat bitter and, as we had still never met, given the difference of our lives and the flux of our existences, I suspected that some external influence or some obscure calculation was to blame, just as do the jealous personae of Proust's novel, gnawed at by the enigma provoked by distance.

Then, suddenly, death—which transformed these letters into a private treasure, a *Tombeau*,[15] an ultimate act of generosity.

When Benoît Chantre, in the name of the Hachette Publishing Company, asked me to write an essay on Deleuze's thought, I said to myself that it was like one last, long posthumous letter. It would not be a matter of my "giving an account"—of describing—what he had thought, but rather of completing the incompletable: a conflictual friendship that, in a certain sense, had never taken place.

O N E

Which Deleuze?

THERE IS an image of Deleuze as, at once, radical and temperate, solitary and convivial, vitalist and democratic. It is fairly commonly believed that his doctrine promotes the heterogeneous multiplicity of desires and encourages their unrestrained realization, that it is concerned with the respect and affirmation of differences, and that it thus constitutes a conceptual critique of totalitarianisms, as is indicated, in practice, by the fact that Deleuze kept his distance—in a way that not even Foucault did—from all Stalinist or Maoist involvements. It is believed that he preserved the rights of the body against terrorizing formalisms; that he made no concession to the spirit of system, but rather constantly commended the Open and movement, advocating an experimentation without preestablished norms. In his method of thinking, which admits only cases and singularities, he is believed to have stood fast against the crushing abstractions of the dialectic. It is equally believed that he participates in modern (postmodern?) "deconstruction," insofar as he carries out a decisive critique of representation, substitutes the logic of sense for the search for truth, and combats transcendent idealities in the name of the creative immanence of life: in sum, that he adds his contribution to the ruin of metaphysics, to the "overturning of Platonism," by promoting, against the sedentary *nomos* of Essences, the nomad *nomos* of precarious actualizations, divergent series, and unpredictable creations. The confirmation of this postmetaphysical modernity is found in the rippling of references: the painters (Francis Bacon), the writers (Proust, Melville, Lewis Carroll, Beckett...), the vicissitudes of desire (Sacher-Masoch), the unexpected philosophers (Whitehead, Tarde, Duns Scotus...), the metaphorized mathematics (Riemann), the innumerable filmmakers, as indeed the numerous authors whom almost no one has ever heard of (except for him), or the vast array of articles or opuscules bearing on obscure questions—dealing with everything from sociology to biology, aesthetics to didactics, and linguistics to history—that he was to rethink and render dazzling. And, indeed, all these references are abruptly drawn together in a sinuous affirmative web that seems far removed from the precautions and canons of the philosophical university.

Finally, Deleuze, curious about every aspect of his time and adjusting both his thought to the capture of the shimmering surface of an event's occurrence and his magical writing to the traversing of meaning's disparate zones, is considered, in echo of the virtue that he conceded to be Leibniz's in the classical age, as the inventor of a contemporary Baroque, in which our desire for the multiple, intermixtures, and the coexistence of universes free of any common rule—in sum, our planetary democratism—is able to recognize itself and unfurl. In short, we end up with Deleuze as the joyous thinker of the world's *confusion*.

A Renewed Concept of the One

Philosophically, the world's confusion undoubtedly means first of all that it can be explained neither by the One nor by the Multiple. This world is not taken up within the identifiable movement of a meaning (for example, the meaning of History), nor does it fall under the regime of stable classifications or practicable analyses into significative components (as it did in the conception of those who clearly distinguished the proletariat from the bourgeoisie, or made sense of the games between imperialist, socialist, and nonaligned camps). And it seems, at first, that Deleuze is indeed he who announces that the distribution of Being according to the One and the Multiple must be renounced, that the inaugural methodological gesture of any modern thought is to situate itself outside this opposition. Repetition is a major ontological concept for him precisely because it cannot be thought as either the permanence of the One or as the multiple of identifiable terms, but is *beyond* this opposition: "Repetition is no more the permanence of the One than the resemblance of the multiple" (*Difference and Repetition*, p. 126; translation modified). More generally, "there is neither one nor multiple" (*Foucault*, p. 14).

But, as always with Deleuze, going beyond a static (quantitative) opposition always turns out to involve the *qualitative* raising up of one of its terms.

And, contrary to the commonly accepted image (Deleuze as liberating the anarchic multiple of desires and errant drifts), contrary even to the apparent indications of his work that play on the opposition multiple/multiplicities ("there are only rare multiplicities"; ibid.), it is the occurrence of the One—renamed by Deleuze the One-All—that forms the supreme destination of thought and to which thought is accordingly consecrated. We only need to heed, paying attention to its enthusiastic vibration even more than to its explicit content, the following declaration: "A single and same voice for the whole thousand-voiced multiple, a single and same Ocean for all the drops, a single clamour of Being for all beings" (*Difference and Repetition*, p. 304). And let us also remind those who naively celebrate a Deleuze for whom everything is event, surprise, and creation that the multiplicity of "what-occurs" is but a misleading surface, because for veritable thought, "Being is the unique event in which all events communicate with one another" (*The Logic of Sense*, p. 180). Being—which is also Sense—is "the position in the void of all events in one, the expression in nonsense of all senses in one" (ibid.; translation modified).

Deleuze's fundamental problem is most certainly not to liberate the multiple but to submit thinking to a renewed concept of the One. What must the One be, for the multiple to be *integrally* conceivable therein as the production of simulacra? Or, yet again: in what way should the All be determined, in order that the existence of each portion of this All—far from being positioned as independent or as surging forth unpredictably—be nothing other than an expressive profile of "the powerful, nonorganic Life that embraces the world?" (*Cinema 2*, p. 81; translation modified).

We can therefore first state that one must carefully identify a metaphysics of the One in the work of Deleuze. He himself indicates what its requisites are: "one single event for all events; a single and same *aliquid* for that which happens and that which is said; and a single and same being for the impossible, the possible and the real" (*The Logic of Sense*, p. 180; translation modified). The real basis of the supposed democracy of desire lies, in fact, in the attaining of this "one single."

The "Purified Automaton"

All those who believe that Deleuze's remarks may be seen to encourage autonomy or the anarchizing ideal of the sovereign individual populating the Earth with the productions of his/her desires are no less mistaken. They do not take literally enough the strictly "*machinic*" conception that Deleuze has, not only of desire (the famous "desiring-machines") but, even more so, of will or choice. For this conception strictly precludes any idea of ourselves as being, at any time, the source of what we think or do. Everything always stems from afar—indeed, everything is always "already-there," in the infinite and inhuman resource of the One.

By way of example, let us examine the theory of choice. The first step is to establish that the stakes of a veritable choice (a choice that Deleuze describes as bearing on "existential determinations"; *Cinema 2*, p. 177) are not the explicit terms of the choice, but the "mode of existence of the one who chooses" (ibid.). From there, one easily passes to the well-known theme of Kierkegaard: an authentic choice is never the choice of this or that; rather, it is the choice to choose, the choice between choosing and not choosing. Detached in this way from any particular stake, choice takes on the form of an "absolute relation with the outside" (ibid.). But what is to be understood by the absoluteness of such a relation? It means that the power of inorganic life operates in us, that we are *traversed* by an actualization of the One-All. As a result, choice is all the more "pure" for being automatic: in reality, we are ourselves chosen, far from being, as the philosophy of representation would have it, the center, or seat, of a decision: "Only he who is chosen chooses well or effectively" (ibid., p. 178). This figure of the automaton, which links up easily with that of the "machinery" that produces sense, represents the veritable subjective ideal, precisely because it demolishes all subjective pretensions. The outside, as agency of active force, takes hold of a body, selects an individual, and submits it to the choice of choosing: "it is precisely the automaton, purified in this way, that thought seizes from the outside, as the unthinkable in thought" (ibid.; translation modified).[1] This "purified automaton" is certainly much closer to the Deleuzian norm than were the bearded militants of 1968, bearing the standard of their gross desire. For, as we have just seen, we are dealing here with the conditions of thought and these are a matter of purification, sobriety, and a concentrated and lucid exposure to the immanent sovereignty of the One. We must, through the sustained renunciation of the obviousness of our needs and occupied positions, attain that empty place where, seized by impersonal powers, we are constrained to make thought exist through us: "Today's task is to make the empty square circulate and to make preindividual and nonpersonal singularities speak" (*The Logic of Sense*, p. 73). Thinking is not the spontaneous effusion of a personal capacity. It is the power, won only with the greatest difficulty *against oneself*, of being constrained to the world's play.

It follows that, contrary to all egalitarian or "communitarian" norms, Deleuze's conception of thought is profoundly aristocratic. Thought only exists in a hierarchized space. This is because, for individuals to attain the point where they are seized by their preindividual determination and, thus, by the power of the One-All—of which they are, at the start, only meager local configurations—

they have to go beyond their limits and endure the transfixion and disintegration of their actuality by infinite virtuality, which is actuality's veritable being. And individuals are not equally capable of this. Admittedly, Being is itself neutral, equal, outside all evaluation, in the sense that Nietzsche declares that the value of life cannot be evaluated. But "things reside unequally in this equal being" (*Difference and Repetition*, p. 37). It is always a question of knowing "whether a being...transcends its limits in going to the limit of what it can do, whatever its degree" (ibid.). And, as a result, it is essential to think according to "a hierarchy which considers things and beings from the point of view of power" (ibid.).

However paradoxical the attribute may seem, applied to someone who claims to draw his inspiration above all from Nietzsche (although there is in Nietzsche himself a profound *saintliness*), it is necessary to uphold that the condition of thought, for Deleuze, is ascetic. This is what radically explains the kinship of Deleuze and the Stoics, other than the fact that they also thought of Being directly as totality. One should not be misled by the use of the word "anarchy" to designate the nomadism of singularities, for Deleuze specifies "crowned anarchy," and it is crucial to think also—indeed, to think above all—the crown. This is attributed to beings who have ascetically renounced the "lived experiences" and "states of affairs" that constituted their sentimental, intellectual, or social actuality and who have had the power to exceed their limits, to go "where they are borne by *hubris*" (ibid.).

The result is that this philosophy of life is essentially, just like Stoicism (but not at all like Spinozism, despite the reverence in which Deleuze holds Spinoza), a philosophy of death. For, if the event of thought is the ascetic power of letting myself be chosen (the Deleuzian form of destiny) and being borne, qua purified automaton, wherever *hubris* carries me; if, therefore, thought exists as the fracturing of my actuality and the dissipation of my limit; but if, at the same time, this actuality and this limit are, in their being, of the same "stuff" as that which fractures and transcends them (given that there is, definitively, only the One-All); and if, therefore, powerful inorganic life is the ground both of what arrays me *in* my limit and of what incites me, insofar as I have conquered the power to do so, to transcend this limit: then it follows that the metaphor for the event of thought is dying, understood as an immanent moment of life. For death is, above all else, that which is *simultaneously* most intimately related to the individual it affects and in a relationship of absolute impersonality or exteriority to this individual. In this sense, it *is* thought, for thinking consists precisely in ascetically attaining that point where the individual is transfixed by the impersonal exteriority that is equally his or her authentic being.

This identity of thinking and dying is declared in a veritable hymn to death, in which Deleuze, slipping effortlessly into the footsteps of Blanchot, exalts "the point at which...the impersonality of dying no longer indicates only the moment when I disappear outside of myself, but rather the moment when death loses itself in itself, and also the figure which the most singular life takes on in order to substitute itself for me" (*The Logic of Sense*, p. 153).

"Monotonous" Productions

That being the case, this philosophy, in which the One is sovereign, the hierarchy of power is ascetic, and death symbolizes thought, can hardly be expected, despite what is often believed, to be devoted to the inexhaustible variety of the concrete.

Certainly, the starting point required by Deleuze's method is always a concrete case. This is what explains that there is no significative difference, for him, between what is, in appearance, a "dogmatic" treatise (*Difference and Repetition*, for example), a text falling within the domain of the history of classical philosophy (*Expressionism in Philosophy: Spinoza*), the dialogue with a great contemporary (*Foucault*), a general survey of a particular art (*Cinema 1* and *Cinema 2*), or a meditation on a writer (*Proust and Signs*). It is always a question of indicating particular *cases of a concept*. If you do not first start with a particular case, you are claiming to go from the concept to the variety that it subsumes. In this way, you reestablish the Platonic transcendence of the Idea, and you show yourself to be unfaithful to the Nietzschean program that, constantly evoked by Deleuze, designates "the overturning of Platonism" as the contemporary philosophical task. Immanence requires that you place yourself where thought has already started, as close as possible to a singular case and to the movement of thought. Thinking happens "behind your back" and you are impelled and constrained by it. And the virtue of the case consists in this.

This also explains something that has often surprised Deleuze's readers: the constant use of the free indirect style, or the deliberate undecidability of "who is speaking?" If I read, for example: "force among forces, man does not fold the forces that compose him without the outside folding itself, and creating a Self within man" (*Foucault*, p. 114), is this really a statement of Foucault's? Or is it already an interpretation? Or is it quite simply a thesis of Deleuze's, for we recognize in these lines his reading of Nietzsche (the play of active and reactive forces typologically *composes* man), just as we note the presence of a major concept of his later works, that of the fold? Rather, one would have to say that this sentence is produced by the impulsion, affecting Deleuze, of that which, in affecting Foucault, was the case of another impulsion, of another constraint. In this sense, given both the dissolution of respective identities and the fact that thinking always consists of making impersonal singularities "speak," one can equally well uphold that the statement in question *becomes* Foucauldian, or that it *will have been* Deleuzian.

But one starts to go wrong as soon as one imagines that the constraint exercised by concrete cases makes of Deleuze's thought a huge description or collection of the diversity characterizing the contemporary world. For one presumes then that the operation consists in thinking the case. This is not so: the case is never an object for thought; rather, intrinsic to the destination that, ultimately automatic, is thought's own, intrinsic to the exercising "to the very end" of thought's power, the case is what forces thought and renders it impersonal. It is therefore perfectly coherent that, in starting from innumerable and seemingly disparate cases, in exposing himself to the impulsion organized by Spinoza and Sacher-Masoch, Carmelo Bene and Whitehead, Melville and Jean-Luc Godard, Francis Bacon and Nietzsche, Deleuze arrives at conceptual productions that I would unhesitatingly qualify as *monotonous*, composing a very particular regime of emphasis or almost infinite repetition of a limited repertoire of concepts, as well as a virtuosic variation of names, under which what is thought remains essentially identical.

The rights of the heterogeneous are, therefore, simultaneously imperative and limited. Thinking can only begin under the violent impulsion of a case-of-thought; that it start off from a principle is excluded. And each beginning, being a singular impulsion, presents also a singular case. But what begins in this way is destined to repetition:[2] the repetition in which the invariable differential of a resource of power takes effect.

Consider the example of cinema. On the one hand, Deleuze singularly analyzes work after work, with the disconcerting erudition of a nonspecialist. Yet, on the other hand, what finally comes out of this is siphoned into the reservoir of concepts that, from the very beginning of his work, Deleuze has established and linked together: namely, movement and time, in the sense that Bergson gives to these terms. Cinema, with its proliferation of films, authors, and tendencies, forms a dynamic and constraining configuration, in which Deleuze comes to occupy the empty place of he who, under the massive power of the case, must, once again, cover the range of his capacities, refashion what he has already produced, and repeat his difference, in differentiating it even more acutely from other differences. This is why film buffs have always found it difficult to make use of the two hefty volumes on the cinema, for, however supple the individual film descriptions may be in their own right, this malleability seems nevertheless to function in philosophy's favor, rather than to fashion, in any way whatsoever, a simple critical judgment that film enthusiasts could draw on to enhance the authority of their opinions.

In effect, Deleuze in no way considers his exposure to cases-of-thought related to the cinema (however thorough this exposure may be) as being equivalent to producing a theory *of* cinema. The end of *Cinema 2* makes it absolutely clear that his entire enterprise is proposing a creative repetition of concepts and not an apprehension of the cinematic art as such: "The theory of cinema does not bear on the cinema, but on the concepts of the cinema" (*Cinema 2*, p. 280). Cinema in itself is "a new practice of images and signs" (ibid.); but thought's objective can in no way be to limit itself to a concrete phenomenology of signs and images. Rather, because "cinema's concepts are not given in cinema," "philosophy must produce the theory [of cinema] as conceptual practice" (ibid.; translation modified). Let us understand that, under the constraint of the case of cinema, it is once again, and always, (Deleuze's) philosophy that begins anew and that causes cinema to be there *where it cannot, of itself, be.*

It is therefore necessary to consider that Deleuze's philosophy is "concrete" only insofar as, in his view, the concept is concrete. This in no way means that the concept is a concept of the concrete; rather, in the same way as with all that is, it marks the impersonal deployments of a local power that is obliged to manifest itself as thought by the concrete cases through which the unique voice of Being makes itself heard in its multiple declension.

When Deleuze sets down that philosophy is a practice and that it is "no more abstract than its object" (ibid.), one has to understand by this that the practice of concepts is neither more nor less concrete than any other practice. But it is impossible to thereby deduce that the concrete multiplicity of cases is what validates the concrete character of a philosophy. When all is said and done, the multiple rippling of cases that are invoked in Deleuze's prose has only an adventitious value. What counts is the impersonal power of the concepts themselves that, in their content, never deal with a "given" concrete instance, but *with other concepts:* "A theory of cinema is not 'about' cinema, but about the concepts that cinema generates" (ibid.; translation modified). The entire interest of these cases lies in this generation, but *what* is generated bears no resemblance to the generating power. Ultimately, concepts, which are never "concepts-of," are only attached to the initial concrete case in their movement and not in what they give to be thought. This is why, in the volumes on the cinema, what one learns concerns the Deleuzian theory of movement and time, and the cinema gradually becomes neutralized and forgotten.

It is therefore necessary to maintain that Deleuze's philosophy is particularly systematic in that all the impulsions are taken in by it according to a line of power that is invariable precisely because it fully assumes its status of singularity. This is why, in my view, it can also be described—at least if the adjective is given a precise meaning—as an abstract philosophy. By "abstraction," one is not to understand that it moves in what it absolutely repudiates: namely, the generality subsuming concrete cases. Let us simply state that the appropriate measure here is the quasi-organic consistency of conceptual connections, and the constant putting into movement of this consistency by the greatest possible number of cases. Care must be taken not to forget that what is submitted to this trial by the adventitious multiple of cases never stops experiencing itself as self-identical. For it is the fact that a concept, traversing the illimited determination of cases, reunites with itself and that it supplely resists the variation of that which calls upon it to return, that constitutes the only possible protocol of validation for this concept.

These, then, are the general principles that govern the examination of Deleuze's philosophy and that, I believe, are both faithful to its spirit and far removed from the *doxa* that has been constituted around it:

1. This philosophy is organized around a metaphysics of the One.

2. It proposes an ethics of thought that requires dispossession and asceticism.

3. It is systematic and abstract.

In my view, the second and third points are virtues more than anything else. The first is complicated and opens onto a *disputatio* that we undertook in the correspondence of which I have spoken. A dispute and not a debate: for, in conformity with his aristocratic and systematic leanings, Deleuze felt only contempt for debates. He set this down in writing—much to the chagrin of certain sensitive souls for whom debate alone attests the homogeneity of philosophy and parliamentary democracy.

Neither Deleuze nor I believe in this homogeneity. Thus it is not a question of debating but of patiently testing the principles that I have just drawn out. For, as far as I am concerned, and given my attempt to redress Platonism rather than overturn it, I am convinced that principles do exist.

T   **W**   **O**

Univocity of Being and
Multiplicity of Names

OUR EPOCH can be said to have been stamped and signed, in philosophy, by the return of the question of Being. This is why it is dominated by Heidegger. He drew up the diagnosis and explicitly took as his subject the realignment, after a century of Criticism and the phenomenological interlude, of thought with its primordial interrogation: what is to be understood by the being of beings?[1] When all is said and done, there is little doubt that the century has been ontological, and that this destiny is far more essential than the "linguistic turn" with which it has been credited. This turn amounts to making language, its structures, and its resources the transcendental of every investigation of the faculty of knowledge, and to the setting up of philosophy as either a generalized grammar or a weak logic. But when we read Wittgenstein, who is the only really great thinker of this turn, we realize that the moment of the most rigorous conceptual tension in the *Tractatus* is when an altogether remarkable ontological base — the theory of eternal objects — has been secured. We also realize that the last word belongs to a silent supracognitive, or mystical, intuition that lies beyond the logical structures to which cognitive propositions are confined and that alone opens us to the question that matters: what ought I to do? If it is true that the limits of the world are exactly the limits of language, the result is that whatever decides the fate of thought, which exceeds the limits of the world, exceeds equally those of language. This implies that, although the validity (or the sense) of scientific propositions (propositions bearing on the representations of such or such a part of the world) can only be assured by the means of the analytic of language (this is the critical residue), it is nevertheless beyond this analytic that thought accords with its highest power, which is that of interrogating the *value* of the world itself. In Wittgenstein, language is undermined by the question concerning Being—if not regarding its uses, at least regarding its *finality*.[2]

In this sense, Deleuze belongs absolutely to this century. His thought can no more be attached to the analytic current, whose grammatical or logicizing reductions he abhors, than it can be to the phenomenological current, which he severely criticizes for its reduction of living actualizations to simple intentional correlations of consciousness.

The question posed by Deleuze is the question of Being. From beginning to end, and under the constraint of innumerable and fortuitous cases, his work is concerned with thinking thought (its act, its movement) on the basis of an ontological precomprehension of Being as One.

It is impossible to overemphasize this point, consistently occulted by critical or phenomenological interpretations of his work: Deleuze purely and simply identifies philosophy with ontology. One misses everything if one disregards such explicit declarations as "Philosophy merges with ontology" (*The Logic of Sense*, p. 179), or "from Parmenides to Heidegger it is the same voice which is taken up.... A single voice raises the clamour of being" (*Difference and Repetition*, p. 35). The historical[3] unifier of philosophy, as the voice of thought, as the clamor of the utterable, is Being itself. From this point of view, Deleuze's philosophy is in no way a critical philosophy. Not only is it possible to think Being, but there is thought only insofar as Being simultaneously formulates and pronounces itself therein. Certainly, thought is difference and identification of differences; it always consists in conceiving of "several formally distinct senses" (ibid.). The thinking impulsion manifests itself as a vital power in plurality (the plurality of senses, of cases); yet Deleuze immediately adds that it is not the formal distinction of the multiple that is important for thought. What is important is that all the senses, all the cases, "refer to ... a single designated entity, ontologically one" (ibid.). In this sense, *every* philosophical proposition is what Deleuze calls "the ontological proposition" (ibid.), which recapitulates a maximal conviction regarding the resource of being that belongs to speech and thought. Parmenides maintained that Being and thought were one and the same thing. The Deleuzian variant of this maxim is: "it is the same thing which occurs and is said" (*The Logic of Sense*, p. 180). Or, yet again: "Univocal being inheres in language and happens to things; it measures the internal relation of language with the external relation of being" (ibid.; translation modified). How very Greek this confidence in Being as the measure of relations, both internal and external, is! And how very indifferent to the "linguistic turn" this ontological coemergence of sentences and what-occurs under the rule of the One is!

Under these conditions, how does Deleuze differ from Heidegger—other, of course, than the evident difference between the prophetic, pathetic, professorial style of the German and the alert sinuousness, the discontinuous scintillation, of the Frenchman? This is an extremely complex question: for my part, I would maintain that Deleuze is, on a number of critical points (difference, the open, time . . .), less distant from Heidegger than is usually believed and than he no doubt believed himself to be. In restricting ourselves to explicit distinctions, we can state that, for Deleuze, Heidegger is still and always too phenomenological. What should we understand by this?

Heidegger's Limit

"Vulgar" phenomenology's initial premise is that consciousness "is directed towards the thing and gains significance in the world" (*Foucault*, p. 108). This is what phenomenology names intentionality. That the thinking of thought (philosophy's unique objective) could start from such a signifying directedness is repugnant to Deleuze for two convergent reasons.

First, consciousness can in no way constitute the immediate starting point for an investigation of thought. Indeed, we know that one begins to think only under a constraint and according to a force, in an ascetic exposure to the impersonal imperative of the outside. Under these conditions, it is not at all in consciousness that thought has its source. In fact, to begin to think, it is necessary to turn away from consciousness, "to become unconscious," one might say. As Deleuze puts it, drawing on Marx, "While it is the nature of consciousness to be false, problems by their nature escape consciousness" (*Difference and Repetition*, p. 208).

Second, and above all, thought is presented by intentionality as dependent on an internalized relation: between consciousness and its object, ideation and the ideatum, the noetic pole and the noematic pole, or, in the Sartrean variant, the for-itself and the in-itself. Yet, precisely because thought is the deployment of the Being-One, its element is never of the order of an internalized relation, representation, or consciousness-of. Thought presupposes that the multiple modalities of Being are mutually external and that no modality can have the privilege (as consciousness claims to have) of internalizing the others. It is the equality of Being that is at stake here, and this equality implies, without any paradox whatsoever, that nothing of what is ever has the slightest *internal* relation to anything else. One can even affirm that the absolute respect of Being as One in fact demands that each of its immanent actualizations is in a state of nonrelation with all the others. Deleuze, under the name of Foucault (or under the constraint of the case-Foucault), indicates, therefore, that seeing and speaking, things and words, constitute registers of being (of thought) that are entirely disjointed: "we do not see what we speak about, nor do we speak about what we see" (*Foucault*, p. 109); the result being that "knowledge is irreducibly double, since it involves speaking and seeing, language and light, which is the reason why there is no intentionality" (ibid.).

Does this not contradict what we recalled earlier—namely, that it is the same thing that occurs and that is said? Not at all. It is exactly because it is the same Being that occurs and that is said that there is no intentional relation *between* things and words—those actualizations of the Same. For were such a relation to exist, there would be an inequality between the active pole (the directedness, the nomination) and the passive pole (the object, the thing said). However, Being "occurs" in the same way in all its modalities—in the visible and language, for example (one could cite others). Thus, in assuming that there is an intentional relation between nomination and the thing, or between consciousness and the object, one necessarily breaks with the expressive sovereignty of the One. Were the objection to be made that these modalities are at least minimally "related" to each other insofar as they are all modalities of the One, one need but reply that the essence of this relation is the nonrelation, for its only content is the neutral equality of the One. And it is, doubtlessly, in the exercise of this nonrelation that thought "relates" most faithfully to the Being that constitutes it. This is what Deleuze calls a "disjunctive synthesis": one has to think the nonrelation according to the One, which, founds it by radically separating the terms involved. One has to steadfastly rest within the activity of separation, understood as a power of Being. One has to explain that "the nonrelation is still a relation, and even a relation of a deeper sort" (ibid., p. 63; translation modified), insofar as it is thought in accordance with the divergent or disjoining movement that, incessantly separating, testifies to the infinite and egalitarian fecundity of the One. But this disjunctive synthesis is the ruin of intentionality.

We can thus clearly state that what Deleuze considered as Heidegger's limit is that his apparent criticism of intentionality in favor of a hermeneutic of Being stops halfway, for it does not attain the radicalness of the disjunctive synthesis. It retains the motif of the relation, even if in sophisticated form.

Certainly, Deleuze acknowledges that Heidegger's move merits esteem: there is a "surpassing of intentionality...towards Being" (ibid., p. 110), just as the consciousness-object (or consciousness-being) relation is subverted by the passage from phenomenology to ontology. And, in keeping with his supposition of the One, Deleuze cannot but approve of the fact that the dissymmetrical couple composed of the reflexive subject and the object, of interiority and exteriority, is replaced by "the unity of the unveiling-veiling" (ibid.).

However, for Deleuze, if Heidegger surpasses intentionality, he simply then goes on to maintain its ontological substratum, consisting of the relation, or community of senses, between the actualized dimensions of Being, in another dimension. It is for this reason, Deleuze declares, that for Heidegger "Light opens up a speaking no less than a seeing, as if signification haunted the visible which in turn murmured meaning" (ibid., p. 111). The unity of Being is interpreted by Heidegger as a hermeneutic convergence, as an analogical relation that can be deciphered between the dimensions (in this case, the visible and language) in which it is revealed. He does not see (unlike Foucault) that the consequence of ontological unity is not a harmony or a communication between beings, nor even an "interval in between" where the relation can be thought outside all substantial grounding, but rather the absolute nonrelation or the indifference of the terms involved to all forms of relation. Despite the pathos with which Heidegger talks of distress, his vision of the manner in which Being deploys itself in divergent series remains fundamentally a tranquil one, precisely because of its hermeneutical reference. Despite his apologetics of the Open, he refolds and closes up all the separations, the differentiations without resemblance, and the unresolved divergences that alone *prove* the equality and neutrality of the One. Heidegger, to adopt a Nietzschean expression, is a conniving priest who only seems to subvert intentionality and consciousness in order to all the more subtly stand in the way of the disjunctive synthesis. Ultimately, he remains within phenomenology, in the sense that phenomenology is "too pacifying and has consecrated too many things" (ibid., p. 113; translation modified).

The real reason for the disparity between Deleuze and Heidegger, within their shared conviction that philosophy rests solely on the question of Being, is the following: for Deleuze, Heidegger does not uphold the fundamental thesis of Being as One *up to its very end*. He does not uphold this because he does not assume the consequences of the *univocity* of Being. Heidegger continually evokes the maxim of Aristotle: "Being is said in various senses,"[4] in various categories. It is impossible for Deleuze to consent to this "various."

The Univocity of Being

This brings us to the very core of Deleuze's thought. It is, in fact, entirely reasonable to maintain that the sole function of the immense pedagogy of cases (cinema, the schizo, Foucault, Riemann, *Capital*, Spinoza, the nomad, and so on) is to verify tirelessly—with the inexhaustible genius of variation—this unique sentence: "There has only ever been one ontological proposition: Being is univocal" (*Difference and Repetition*, p. 35; *see the selection of texts at the end of this book* [Appendix: "The Univocity of Being (I)" and "The Univocity of Being (II)"]). When Deleuze affirms the identity of philosophy and ontology, he adds in the same sentence that "ontology merges with the univocity of Being" (*The Logic of Sense*, p. 179).[5]

What is to be understood by this decisive univocity? This is what the whole of the present text wants to elucidate, even if it will probably prove to be insufficient.

Let us adopt an external viewpoint. The thesis of the univocity of Being guides Deleuze's entire relation to the history of philosophy. His companions, his references, his preferred cases-of-thought are indeed found in those who have explicitly maintained that being has "a single voice": Duns Scotus, who is perhaps the most radical ("There has only ever been one ontology, that of Duns Scotus"; *Difference and Repetition*, p. 35); the Stoics, who referred their doctrine of the proposition to the contingent coherence of the One-All; Spinoza, obviously, for whom the unity of Substance barred the way to any and all ontological equivocity; Nietzsche, who was to "realize univocity in the form of repetition in the eternal return" (ibid., p. 304);[6] Bergson, for whom all instances of organic differentiation are the expression, in a single sense, of a local actuality of Creative Evolution. It is therefore possible to "read" historically the thesis of univocity, and this is indeed why Deleuze became the (apparent) historian of certain philosophers: they were cases of the univocity of Being.

This reading allows us to formulate two abstract theses in which this principle is unfolded:

Thesis 1: In the first place, univocity does not signify that being is numerically one, which is an empty assertion. The One is not here the one of identity or of number, and thought has already abdicated if it supposes that there is a single and same Being. The power of the One is much rather that "beings are multiple and different, they are always produced by a disjunctive synthesis, and they themselves are disjointed and divergent, *membra disjoncta*" (*The Logic of Sense*, p. 179). Nor does univocity mean that thought is tautological (the One is the One). Rather, it is fully compatible with the existence of multiple *forms* of Being. Indeed, it is even in the power of deployment of these multiple forms that the One can be identified: this is true of Spinoza's Substance, which is immediately expressed by an infinity of attributes. But the plurality of forms does not involve any "division within Being or plurality of ontological senses" (*Difference and Repetition*, p. 303).[7] In other words, it is in a single and same sense that Being is said of all its forms. Or, yet again: the immanent attributes of Being that express its infinite power of One "are *formally* distinct [but] they all remain equal and *ontologically* one" (ibid.). We should note that this thesis already supposes a critical distinction, the importance of which is usually underestimated when one speaks about Deleuze, despite the fact that, conceptually, it alone explains the relation (qua nonrelation) between the multiple and the one: the distinction of the formal and the real. The multiple acceptations of being must be understood as a multiple that is formal, while the One alone is real, and only the real supports the distribution of sense (which is unique).

Thesis 2: In each form of Being, there are to be found "individuating differences" that may well be named beings. But these differences, these beings, never have the fixedness or the power of distribution and classification that may be attributed, for example, to species or generalities, or even individuals, if we understand by "individual" something that can be thought under a species, a generality, or a type. For Deleuze, beings are local degrees of intensity or inflections of power that are in constant movement and entirely singular. And as power is but a name of Being, beings are only expressive modalities of the One. From this it follows once again that the numerical distinction between beings "is a modal, not a real, distinction" (ibid., p. 304). In other words, it is obvious that we have to recognize that beings are not the same and that they therefore do not have the same sense. We have to admit an equivocity of *that of which* Being is said: its immanent modalities, that is, beings. But this is not what is fundamental for the philosopher. What is fundamental is that Being is the same for all, that it is univocal and that it is thus said of all beings in a single and same sense, such that the multiplicity of senses, the equivocal status of beings, has no real status. For the univocity of Being is not solely, nor even principally, the fact that what is "designated" by the diversity of senses of beings is necessarily the same (the Being-One). Univocity requires that the sense be *ontologically identical* for all the different beings: "In the ontological proposition...the sense, too, is ontologically the same for individuating modes, for numerically distinct designators or expressors" (ibid., pp. 35–36; translation modified). Or, yet again: "The univocity of Being signifies...that it is said in one and the same 'sense' of everything of which it is said" (*The Logic of Sense*, p. 179; translation modified).[8]

The price one must pay for inflexibly maintaining the thesis of univocity is clear: given that the multiple (of beings, of significations) is arrayed in the universe by way of a numerical difference that is purely formal as regards the form of being to which it refers (thought, extension, time, etc.) and purely modal as regards its individuation, it follows that, ultimately, this multiple can only be of the order of simulacra. And if one classes — as one should — every difference without a real status, every multiplicity whose ontological status is that of the One, as a simulacrum, then the world of beings is the theater of the simulacra of Being.

Strangely, this consequence has a Platonic, or even Neoplatonic, air to it. It is as though the paradoxical or supereminent One immanently engenders a procession of beings whose univocal sense it distributes, while they refer to its power and have only a semblance of being. But, in this case, what meaning is to be given to the Nietzschean program that Deleuze constantly validates: the overturning of Platonism?

The Multiplicity of Names

This question is explicitly answered by Deleuze: "Consequently, 'to overturn Platonism' means to make the simulacra rise and to affirm their rights" (ibid., p. 262; translation modified). Deleuzianism is fundamentally a Platonism with a different accentuation. Certainly, it is true that sense is distributed according to the One and that beings are of the order of simulacra. And it is no less certain that the fact of thinking beings as simulacra presupposes that one understands the way (what Plato names "participation") in which the individuating differences are arranged in degrees, which "immediately relate them to univocal Being" (*Difference and Repetition*, p. 303).[9] But it in no way follows from this, as Deleuze assumes is the case with Plato, that the simulacra or beings are necessarily depreciated or considered as nonbeings. On the contrary, it is necessary to affirm the rights of simulacra as *so many equivocal cases of univocity* that joyously attest to the univocal power of Being. What Deleuze believes he adds to Plato here, and that, in his eyes, subverts or overturns the latter, is that it is futile to claim that the simulacra are unequal to some supposed model, or that there is a hierarchy in Being that would subordinate the simulacra to real archetypes. Here again, Deleuze suspects Plato of not firmly upholding the thesis of ontological univocity. If Being is said in one and the same sense of everything of which it is said, then beings are all identically simulacra and all affirm, by an inflection of intensity whose difference is purely formal or modal, the living power of the One. Once again, it is the disjunctive synthesis that is opposed to Plato: beings are merely disjointed, divergent simulacra that lack any internal relation between themselves or with any transcendent Idea whatsoever. Conceived as the immanent production of the One, the world is thus, in the same way as for Plato, a work and not a state. It is demiurgic. But the "non-hierarchized work is a condensation of coexistences and a simultaneity of events" (*The Logic of Sense*, p. 262). One does far more justice to the real One by thinking the egalitarian coexistence of simulacra in a positive way than by opposing simulacra to the real that they lack, in the way Plato opposes the sensible and the intelligible. For, in fact, this real lies nowhere else than *in that which founds the nature of the simulacrum as simulacrum*: the purely formal or modal character of the difference that constitutes it, from the viewpoint of the univocal real of Being that supports this difference within itself and distributes to it a single sense.

I am not sure that Plato is so far from this view of beings, even sensible beings, as immanent differentiations of the intelligible and as positivities of the simulacrum. One is struck by the way that Socrates' interlocutors ironically punctuate the transcendence of the Good in the *Republic*, and even more by the way, in the *Parmenides*, that the definition of the status as such of the One only proves capable of unraveling its relation with the others-than-the-One within a register of paradox and impasse. The only way of extricating oneself from such chicanery is to propose a status of pure event for the One, and at that moment one is in attunement with Deleuze when he writes: "Only the free man, therefore, can comprehend all violence in a single act of violence, and every mortal event *in a single Event*" (ibid., p. 152). One wonders whether this Event with a capital "E" might not be Deleuze's Good. In light of the way it requires and founds the temperament of "the free man," this would seem probable.

But, even in supposing that the glorification of simulacra as a positive dimension of the univocity of Being constitutes an overturning of Platonism, the fact remains that, in the same way as for Plato (with all the chicanery of the Idea, of the Good that "is not an Idea," of the Beautiful that is the Good but cannot be confused with it, of the Other which requires that the transcendent unity of the Good be sacrificed, of the One that can neither be nor not be, etc.), Deleuze's approach has to confront the thorny question of the names of Being. What, indeed, could be the appropriate name for that which is univocal? Is the nomination of the univocal itself univocal? And if Being is said in a single sense, how is the sense of this "single sense" to be determined? Or, yet again: is it possible to experiment, to test whether a name of Being makes sense of univocal sense?

Deleuze begins with an uncontroversial declaration: "We can conceive that names or propositions do not have the same sense even while they designate exactly the same thing.... The distinction between these senses is indeed a real distinction (*distinctio realis*), but there is nothing numerical—much less ontological—about it; it is a formal, qualitative or semiological distinction" (*Difference and Repetition*, p. 35). However, when it is a question of Being, we cannot content ourselves with a formal distinction between the senses of names, for the essential property of Being is precisely not its numerical identity, to which different nominal unities—each with its own sense—could refer, but its being said in a single sense of everything of which it is said. In an inevitably paradoxical way, the question of the name of Being persists.

With the exception of "Being," which is not a "name" and which, moreover, Deleuze only uses in a preliminary and limited manner, we can only experiment with the values of names. This means that in a considerable part of his work, Deleuze adopts a procedure that, starting from the constraint exercised by a particular case-of-thought—it does not matter whether this concerns Foucault or Sacher-Masoch—consists in trying out a name of Being and in constructing a protocol of thought (that is to be as automatic as possible) by which the pertinence of this name can be evaluated with respect to the essential property that one expects it to preserve (or even to reinforce within thought): namely, univocity.

What emerges over the course of these experiments is that a single name is never sufficient, but that two are required. Why? The reason is that Being needs to be said in a single sense both from the viewpoint of the unity of its power and from the viewpoint of the multiplicity of the divergent simulacra that this power actualizes in itself. Ontologically, a real distinction is no more involved here than, in Spinoza, between *natura naturans* and *natura naturata*. Yet, a binary distribution of names is necessary; it is as though the univocity of being is thereby accentuated for thought through its being said, at one moment, in its immediate "matter," and, in the next, in its forms or actualizations. In short: in order to say that there is a single sense, two names are necessary.

This problem is constant from Plato (who preliminarily distinguishes the sensible and the intelligible, but as a way of attaining the One) to Heidegger (who marks the difference between being and beings, but as a way of attaining the *destining* or the *Ereignis*). What is particular to Deleuze is that, in conformity with his experimental style of testing concepts under the constraint of cases that vary as much as possible, he proposes a fairly wide array of paired concepts so as to determine the nomination of Being as an interval or nominal interface. It would be false, however, to state that there are as many pairs of names as there are cases. An exhaustive inventory would show that the thesis of univocity is said in ten or so fundamental pairs at most. Compared, however, with the great philosophies recognized by the tradition, this still amounts to a lot. In part, Deleuze's genius—but also the misinterpretations that his philosophy is open to (as a thought of the anarchic multiple of desires, etc.)—is linked to this multiplicity of names of Being, which is itself correlative with the unprecedented determination with which he upholds the ontological thesis of univocity and the fictive character of the multiple. For it is by the experimentation with as many nominal doublets as is necessary that the verification, under constraint, of the absolute unity of sense is wrought.

      After a preliminary exposition of Deleuze's constructive method, I will go on to examine, in the following chapters, what I consider the principal doublets: the virtual and the actual (doctrine of the event); time and truth (doctrine of knowledge); chance and the eternal return (doctrine of action); the fold and the outside (doctrine of the subject).

      Throughout these different stages, I will be concerned with establishing that, whatever the names that might be involved, and given that sense has always already been distributed by Being, Deleuze considers it necessary to entrust oneself to pure affirmation and to take up a stance, in renouncing the simulacrum of oneself, where sense can choose and transfix us, by a gesture unknown to ourselves: "thinking is a throw of the dice" (*Foucault*, p. 117; translation modified).

T H R E E

Method

An Antidialectic

How should we set about thinking a being? Or rather, how are we to approach Being in thinking under the creative constraint of singular beings? We know that "things are deployed across the entire extensity of a univocal and undistributed Being" (*Difference and Repetition*, pp. 36–37). Thought cannot, therefore, ontologically grasp the deployment of things by first instituting a division, or a fixed frame within which beings would be distributed, in such a way that it would be possible to eventually delimit the Being of beings by effecting successive divisions. Deleuze argued throughout his entire work against this kind of procedure, which he named a "sedentary *nomos*" or analogy and in which we can recognize as much the Platonic method of binary divisions (such as that used, in the *Sophist*, to define the angler) as the Hegelian dialectic, in which all the different types of beings are ascribed a place, or a time, in the ordered development of the absolute Idea. For Plato, as for Hegel, thought imposes upon Being a division or a dissymmetrical distribution of its forms, and thinking amounts to methodically running through this distribution. Even Heidegger does not escape the sedentary *nomos*, insofar as Being for him is distributed essentially according to the equivocal division between *phusis* and *technē*.

The attempt to think Being according to a fixed and unequal distribution of its forms has as its operator what Deleuze (following Aristotle) calls categories. A category is the name that is proper to a territory of Being (for example, matter, form, substance, or accident, etc.); but it can equally apply to one of the senses of Being, for all fixedness of the ontological division entails the ruin of univocity. Whoever thinks by categories maintains by this very fact that Being is said in several senses (according to essence or existence, as Idea or as simulacrum, etc.). Conversely, if Being can only be said in a single sense, then it is impossible to think by categories.

We can imagine, however, that thought might in some way approximate the nomadism of Being—the errant movement of its univocity in the absolute equality of simulacra—by multiplying the categories and by infinitely refining the divisions. A singular being would then be like a crossroads of distributions that, although admittedly fixed (for how could one think without a certain stability of categorical divisions?), would be so numerous that they would end up imitating the pure expressive movement of Being in its immanent productions. Such a use of categories would simply be a means of rendering thought supple or flexible and of infinitizing it, instead of restricting oneself, as does Plato (with the sensible and the intelligible, the Idea and the simulacrum) or Hegel (immediacy, externalization, then negative internalization), to a few formal distributions that effectively impede univocity.

With his characteristic rigor and ascetic voluntarism, Deleuze refrains from taking this path: "The list of categories may well be 'opened up' or representation may be made infinite; nevertheless, Being continues to be said in several senses according to the categories, and that of which it is said is determined only by differences 'in general'" (*Difference and Repetition*, p. 303).[1] The true philosophical method must absolutely refrain from any dividing up of the sense of Being by categorical distributions, or from any approximation of its movement by preliminary formal divisions, however refined these may be. The univocity of Being and the equivocity of beings (the latter being nothing other than the *immanent production* of the former) must be thought "together" without the mediation of genera or species, types or emblems: in short, without categories, without generalities.

Deleuze's method is thus a method that rejects all recourse to mediations; indeed, this is why it is essentially antidialectical. Mediation is an exemplary category; supposedly, it enables the passage from one being to another "under" a relation that is internal to at least one of the two. For Hegel, for example, this internalized relation is the negative. However, insofar as univocal Being is affirmation through and through, the negative is totally impossible. In introducing the negative into Being, one ends up with equivocity and, in particular, with the most ancient of its variants—the one that, for Deleuze, defines the "long error," which consists in proclaiming that Being is said according to the sense of its identity and according to the sense of its nonidentity, that it is said as Being and/or as Nothingness. These are the famous "two paths" of Parmenides (the path that affirms Being and that which affirms Non-being). But Deleuze immediately raises the objection that "There are not two 'paths', as Parmenides' poem suggests, but a single 'voice' of Being which includes all its modes, including the most diverse, the most varied, the most differenciated" (ibid., p. 36). The dialectical method, as a method of mediations that claims to internalize the negative, merely partakes of this interminable error.

That being the case, one might be tempted to remark that, although the sedentary distribution of Being and Non-Being is no doubt inappropriate and thought can only speak in "a single voice," don't we nevertheless have to grant at least a certain degree of validity to the categorical opposition of the active and the passive? After all, Spinoza himself, whom Deleuze and Guattari do not hesitate to name the Christ of philosophy, puts this opposition into effect throughout his entire enterprise, from the global figure of the opposition between *natura naturans* and *natura naturata*, to the distinction between the passions that increase our power (joy) and those that diminish it (sadness). One has at least to distribute in a stable way the affirmative and univocal integrity of Being, on the one hand, and that in which, within itself, Being occurs — namely, the separation or equivocal disjunction of beings — on the other. One has to think the active aspect of things (the aspect consisting of singular differentiations or divergent simulacra of univocal Being) separately from their passive aspect (consisting of actual beings, or numerically distinct states of affairs, rendered by equivocal significations).

This duality clearly runs throughout Deleuze's entire work. One could draw up an endless list of the conceptual couples that are organized according to this paramount formal opposition of the active and the passive: the virtual and the actual, inorganic life and species, the schizophrenic and the paranoiac, mass movements and the Party, deterritorialization and reterritorialization, the nomadic and the sedentary, Nietzsche and Plato, the concept and the category, desire and *ressentiment*, spaces of liberty and the State, the statement and the judgment, the body without organs and the fetish, sculpture and theater. . . . Indeed, Deleuze's real method has even been believed to consist ultimately in the play of this formal couple, invested in the thought of contemporary singularities — with this method thus considered as allowing us to discern the liberating path of desiring affirmation and to repudiate the path of passive alienation.

This, however, is not at all the case. The active/passive duality indisputably exercises a strong influence on Deleuze's philosophical language or, let's say, his spontaneous rhetoric. Nonetheless, it is just as unquestionable that Deleuze does everything in his power to escape from this influence. The combat that is Deleuze's—which, as always, is a combat against oneself—is waged precisely, as regards method, on this point: one must strive to ensure that the manner of conducting an analytic that is apparently played out, now on the univocal face of Being (activity), and now on the face of the equivocal multiple of beings (passivity), is never categorical. One must never distribute or divide Being according to these two paths. One must never lose sight of the fact that, if, as we have shown, two names are always necessary to do univocity justice, these two names never operate any ontological division.

The terms that method must obey are explicit: "Neither active nor passive, univocal Being is neutral" (*The Logic of Sense*, p. 180).[2] When thought relies on an analytic in which there is an apparent distribution of the active actualizations of Being and the actual, passive results of these actualizations, the movement of this thought is still incomplete and deficient. Thought can only be sure of itself when it attains the neutral point where activity and passivity are bound by the ontological distribution of an indivisible sense and the simulacra (beings) are thus restored to their egalitarian errant movement, which neutralizes all dialectical opposition *within them* and withdraws them from all internal relations (and thereby from all passivity, as well as from all activity).

In the same way as with all that is, thought is evaluated according to its capacity to go right to the very end, to the limit, of the power that is proper to it and that is forcibly set into motion by the instance of a case-of-thought. But it is necessary to begin somewhere. And, in the initial confusion that we are exposed to by the violence done to us, and without which we would never think, we always begin by a categorical distribution of some kind or by blind judgments that distribute the cases in forms where the univocity of Being is lost. So it is that, in Deleuze's own work, this beginning is often by premature attributions as active and as passive. For example, it is surely insufficient to say of an event that "there are . . . two accomplishments, which are like effectuation and counter-effectuation" (ibid., p. 152; translation modified). Clearly, this emphasis on the Two is purely introductory and still remains within the confines of the categorical. Once this initial formalism is in place, the method consists precisely in fashioning its nomadic subversion and in showing that every relation and every fixed distribution must therefore, insofar as they are indifferent to the terms that are arrayed within them, dissolve and cause thought to return to the neutrality of what Deleuze calls "extra-being."

The Trajectory of the Intuition

A thought without mediation, a thought constructing its movement beyond all the categorical divisions that it has at first been tempted to use as a means of protecting itself from the inhuman neutrality of Being, can only be—as Bergson so sovereignly set down—an intuitive thought. Deleuze's method is the transposition in writing of a singular form of intuition.

Above all, Deleuze's intuition must not be confused with the intuition of the classics and, in particular, with that of Descartes—who, just like Plato and Hegel, is another adversary, another brilliant supporter of the "long error," an upholder of the categories and an enemy of the disjunctive synthesis. As the immediate apprehension of a clear and distinct idea, intuition consists for Descartes in an instantaneous isolation of the idea guided by a localized mental light and free of any connection with any form of obscure ground whatsoever.[3] It is an atom of thought—when one is certain *"uno intuitu,"* in a single "glance." This kind of intuition is based on a theory of natural light that has as its principle that an idea is all the more distinct the clearer it is: "clarity-distinctness constitutes the light which renders thought possible in the common exercise of all the faculties" (*Difference and Repetition*, p. 213). But if beings (or ideas) are only moving inflections of univocal Being, how can they be isolated in this way—in the name of their clarity—from the obscure and all-encompassing "ground" that bears them? Clarity is only a brilliance, that is, a transient *intensity*, and this intensity, being that of a modality of the One, bears in itself the indistinctness of sense. Clarity is thus a punctual concentration of the confused. Conversely, a being that is distinct is a being that is grasped at too great a "distance" from univocity and refolded upon its own sense in such a way that it no longer appears to be a simulacrum as such, for it is cut off (by the so-called Cartesian intuition) from its ontological root. This means that its intensity is minimal and that it cannot possibly be intuited as a clear datum. Distinctness yields to the obscurity of equivocity. It is for this reason that, in radicalizing Leibniz's view that nothing is ever isolated from the all-encompassing murmuring of Being, Deleuze resolutely raises against Descartes's clear and distinct idea the objection that "the clear is in itself confused and the distinct in itself obscure" (ibid.; translation modified).

Intuition's meaning then changes completely. For an intuition that grasps the "distinct-obscure which corresponds to the clear-confused" (ibid.) certainly cannot arise from a single instantaneous glance. It has to plunge into the clear intensity to grasp its confused-being, and revive the "deadened" distinctness of the separated being by uncovering what of it remains obscure: namely, the living immersion that is precisely dissimulated by its isolation. This is why Deleuzian in-tuition is neither a momentary glance of the soul nor a mental atom, but an athletic trajectory of thought and an open multiplicity, just as it is in no way a unilateral movement (a light directed at the thing) but a complex construction that Deleuze frequently names a "perpetual reconcatenation."

Why a "reconcatenation"? We broach here the most difficult aspect of Deleuzian intuition, for this has to be understood as accomplishing, with-out mediation and in a single trajectory, a *double movement*—which has, moreover, already been signaled in the pairing of the clear-confused and the distinct-obscure. On the one hand, Deleuzian intuition has to apprehend the separation of beings as disjunctive synthesis, divergence and equivocity, and so avoid succumbing to the sirens of the categories or to the tranquil classification of beings under generalities that rescind the univocity of Being. But it must also equally think separated beings as simulacra that are purely modal or formal, and thus, ultimately, unseparated in their being, for they are merely local intensities of the One. The result of this is that intuition (as a double movement and, in the final analysis, as writing, as *style*) must simultaneously descend from a singular being toward its active dissolution in the One—thereby presenting it in its being qua simulacrum—and reascend from the One toward the singular being, in following the immanent productive lines of power, and thereby presenting the being in question as a simulacrum of Being. For Deleuze, every construction of thought goes from A to B, then from B to A. But "we do not arrive back at the point of departure as in a bare repetition; rather, the repetition between A and B and B and A is the progressive trajectory or description of the whole of a problematic field" (ibid., p. 210; translation modified). Intuition is what runs through (ideally, at infinite speed) this descent and ascent, in a single cir-cuit. It is indeed a "progressive description of the whole" and is more like a narra-tive adventure than Descartes's instantaneous glance. From A-beings to B-Being, then from B-Being to A-beings, it reconcatenates thought to beings as the copres-ence of a being of the simulacrum and of a simulacrum of Being.

It is necessary to intuit that "every object is double without it being the case that the two halves resemble one another" (ibid., p. 209). Thought is completed when, under the constraint of a case, it has succeeded in thoroughly un-folding that duplicity of beings which is simply the formal expression of the fact that univocity is expressed as equivocity.

As an example, let us consider the signifying phenomena taken up by the structuralism of the sixties: speech acts for the linguists, symptomatic dreams for the psychoanalysts, kinship structures for the anthropologists, and so on. The entire question is how sense is *produced*. Deleuze was delighted by this approach, for each multiplicity of sense can indeed only be (an equivocal) production that is itself distributed by the univocity of the One-All. For him, "sense is never a principle or an origin, . . . it is produced" (*The Logic of Sense*, p. 72; *see the selection of texts* [Appendix: "Sense and the Task of Philosophy"]).

Structuralist thought's first move is to identify each being and each phenomenon, considered as a multiplicity of discrete elements that are themselves subject to preexistent rules of contrast or of position (phonemes of a language, metaphors of a dream, formal groups of the exchange of women, etc.). The simulacral dimension of the entities under consideration is brought to its peak by this combinatory description, for everything seems to be disseminated in a static abstraction: there are only distinct entities. At the same time, this distinctness is obscure insofar as the relation it bears to sense (which it is supposed to support) is entirely problematic. The Structure, consisting of the interrelation of the distinct entities, remains in itself opaque, thwarting all attempts at interpretation. We are in the distinct-obscure.

The second move consists in identifying within the structure a singular entity, which renders it incomplete and sets it into motion: namely, an "empty square" or, as Deleuze puts it, in doing the tour of the principal branches of structuralism (we can recognize, in passing, Jakobson, Lévi-Strauss, Lacan, and Althusser), "the place of the dummy, the place of the king, the blind spot, the floating signifier, the value degree zero, the off-stage or absent cause, etc." (ibid., p. 71). The dynamic capacity of the combinatory ensemble results from the constant putting into play of this empty square, as regards what will come to occupy it. It then becomes possible to think of the structure as a machine to produce sense because (in Deleuze's view) this singular entity *opens it up* to movement and shifts the distinct toward its obscure double, which is signaled, in the positivity of terms and rules, by a gap or lack, a supplement or a paradox, which is the principle of mobility and of production. We are now in the dissolving descent from the structural Full toward the Open of being.

The paradoxical entity shines with a singular brilliance. It is what is fascinating in structuralist theory because it is like a line of flight, an evasion, or an errant liberty, by which one escapes the positivism of legalized beings. In the somber opacity of the combinatory ensemble, it is like a window. The paradoxical entity is a clear singularity. But this clarity equally plunges the whole Structure into confusion, for it is ultimately impossible to render this singularity really distinct. Constantly circulating—like the slipper or handkerchief passed around in certain games—it is always oblique: it is a presence made of absence, a number woven out of vacuity, an active zero, a signifier that does not signify. This means that thought intuits here the clear-confused and leads away from disjunctive separation, in opening up a breach toward univocity. But this also means, with regard to the sense produced by the structure, that thought pays the price of nonsense as the condition for this production. Basically, the empty square shows that the structure is only a simulacrum and that, while it fabricates sense, the being that is proper to it—namely, the life that sustains the effect of sense—does not, in any way, enter into the sense so fabricated. For life (the One), being univocal, holds the equivocity of produced sense for a nonsense.

It is then that the reascent begins. Structuralism, which is only an analysis of beings, is incapable of this movement that consists in thinking how it comes about that nonsense is required to produce sense. Only the thesis of univocity can shed light on this point for, if Being is said in a single sense of all of which it is said, then, from the viewpoint of the multiple universe of the senses produced by the structural machines, *this* (single) sense is inevitably determined as nonsense. No structural machine is capable of producing this sense, which, on the contrary, is what supports (under the stamp of the paradoxical entity) the possibility of production of the former as such. Were a singular configuration capable of producing the sense of Being, then this would entail that there was a sense of sense, which is a specifically theological thesis alien to ontology and spelling the ruin of univocity. From the fact that there is no sense of sense, it is necessary to conclude that the sense of Being can perfectly well be said to be nonsense—provided that we add that sense comes from nonsense, nonsense being precisely the univocal donation of (ontological) sense to all beings.

Deleuze affirms that the constructions of structuralism have legitimately recognized "that sense is produced by nonsense and its perpetual displacement, and that it is born of the respective position of elements which are not by themselves 'signifying'" (ibid., p. 72). However, this thought is still only one of the aspects of the question: namely, the aspect governing the first trajectory of the intuition that descends from the simulacra that induce equivocal sense toward the univocity of nonsense. In order to complete this intuition and thereby bring the construction of thought to its term, we have to grasp the necessity of going *positively* from nonsense to sense, by understanding that nonsense is nothing other than the univocity of Being and that therefore, far from meaning "absence of sense," it is in fact just the opposite, incessantly producing an infinity of senses in the form of simulacra, or modes of its own surface: "Nonsense is that which has no sense but, as such, in enacting the donation of sense, is also the very opposite of the absence of sense" (ibid., p. 71; translation modified). We might as well say that nonsense *is* ontologically sense, for we know that the One is life or production and that, consequently, the univocal sense of Being is only effective as the *donation* of sense.

Philosophical intuition is now, under the injunction of the case-of-structuralism, the integral and integrated trajectory of the following two types of statements:

- descending, or analytic, statements: "there are different senses"; "they are produced by combinatory machines"; "these machines are open at the singular point of the empty square"; "sense is produced by nonsense";

- ascending, or productive, statements: "Being is univocal"; "it cannot make sense by itself, because there is no sense of sense"; "it is therefore nonsense"; "this nonsense is the donation of (ontological) sense"; "there are different senses qua machinic simulacra of the univocity of Being (of nonsense qua the name of sense as what *occurs* multiply in beings)."

The whole problem consists in maintaining the unity of the trajectory and in not letting it fall back into categorical forms that would divide up Being. Effectively, this is a risk we run in employing the images of descending and reascending, especially in that Deleuze, being a good Nietzschean, refuses any vertical dimension to sense. Sense "belongs to no height or depth, but rather to a surface effect, being inseparable from the surface which is its proper dimension" (ibid., p. 72). It will be agreed that, here, "ascending" and descending" are only the obligatory pair of names required to name what the being of a thought is: *an* intuition, which is, integrally and completely, a movement of and within the surface, or, in other words, a violent *superficial tension.*

But it is perhaps under the impulsion of the case-Bergson that Deleuze best expresses the integrated double movement of his intuitive method. Deleuze is a marvelous reader of Bergson, who, in my opinion, is his real master, far more than Spinoza, or perhaps even Nietzsche. Let us therefore expose ourselves to the injunction of Bergson and ask what is movement. This requires that we distinguish three levels: first, the objects (closed sets) that are precisely defined by their distinct (and therefore opaque or obscure) character; second, the elementary movement of translation that modifies the position of objects and of which we have an immediate or spatial experience that is clear (and thus confused); and finally, the

Whole,[4] or the duration, that, constantly changing, is a spiritual reality (which means that it is neither distributed nor divided, but is nonsense as the univocal production of the equivocal sense of objects).

It is then necessary to state that "movement has two aspects . . . , that which happens between objects or parts [and] that which expresses the duration or the whole" (*Cinema 1*, p. 11; *see the selection of texts* [Appendix: "Movement and Multiplicities"]). We recognize here the elementary distinction between the patent character of simulacra and their expressive value from the viewpoint of the One. The double trajectory, given in the philosophical intuition of movement, will be expressed as the active undoing of this distinction or as the thought of the two aspects of movement as depending on *a* duplicity. What we have to think here is, in fact, that movement "relates the objects of a closed system to open duration [this will be recognized as the descending dimension of intuition, from beings toward Being] and duration to the objects of the system which it forces to open up [this will be recognized as the ascending dimension, from Being toward beings]" (ibid.).

But on what grounds can this double trajectory designate *an* intuition? It is here that we doubtlessly find the most profound idea of Bergson-Deleuze: *when we have grasped the double movement of descent and ascent, from beings to Being, then from Being to beings, we have in fact thought the movement of Being itself, which is only the interval, or the difference, between these two movements.* As Deleuze writes: "Through movement the whole is divided up into objects, and objects are re-united in the whole, and indeed between the two 'the whole' changes" (ibid.). Univocal Being is indeed nothing other than, at one and the same time, the superficial movement of its simulacra *and* the ontological identity of their intensities: it is, simultaneously, nonsense and the universal donation of sense. If thought seizes hold of these two aspects, which necessitates that it be the movement of two movements, it is adequate to Being.

We can now conclude concerning the intuitive method of Deleuze. When thought succeeds in constructing, without categories, the looped path that leads, on the surface of what is, from a case to the One, then from the One to the case, it intuits the movement of the One itself. And because the One *is* its own movement (because it is life, or infinite virtuality), thought intuits the One. It thereby, as Spinoza so magnificently expressed it, attains intellectual beatitude, which is the enjoyment of the Impersonal.[5]

F   O   U   R

The Virtual

"VIRTUAL" IS without any doubt the principal name of Being in Deleuze's work. Or rather, the nominal pair virtual/actual exhausts the deployment of univocal Being. But we are now familiar with the Deleuzian logic of the One: two names are required for the One *in order to test that the ontological univocity designated by the nominal pair proceeds from a single one of these names*. We require the couple virtual/actual to test that an actual being univocally possesses its being as a function of its virtuality. In this sense, the virtual is the ground of the actual.

        The objection will be made that Deleuze, as a modern philosopher, repudiates the notion of ground. Is it not a major characteristic of all contemporary thought to challenge the theme of the ground [*fond*], of grounding, of foundation? Do we not see declarations spring up everywhere concerning the "groundless ground" [*fond sans fond*], the withdrawal of any form of grounding, the pure "thrownness" of the human being, the abyss, the inexistence of any destining source, the desolation of the primordial earth, the loss of sense, the inevitable nihilism? Like all of us, Deleuze takes part in this concert, and does not balk at the punning on the root "*fond*" that this kind of exercise engenders.[1] He declares, for example, concerning the simulacrum and its affirmative, anti-Platonic sovereignty, that, "far from being a new ground [*fondement*], it engulfs all grounds, it assures a universal caving-in [*effondrement*], but as a joyful and positive event, as an *un-grounding* [*effondement*]" (*The Logic of Sense*, p. 263; translation modified).

We can well understand that the Deleuzian (Nietzschean) discovery of beings as merely superficial intensities of simulacra of Being seems to relieve thought of all pathos concerning the ground. For it is indeed possible to give a restricted version of the idea of ground. Whenever beings are posed as copies of a form of Being (in the sense that the Platonic sensible is an image of the intelligible, or that man is created "in the image of" God for the Scriptures), what is involved is the simultaneously theoretical and moral injunction to return to the real principle of the copy, the ideal Model, as that which founds the play of appearances. The quest for the ground is thus linked to a *mimetic* vision of being. And this vision has two consequences: on the one hand, there is a necessary equivocity of Being, according to whether it is said of the real ground [*fond*], the paradigm, or of the imitations, whereas, on the other hand, thought is necessarily categorical, for it has to distribute Being according to that which is the same as the ground, and according to that which only resembles it. Understood in this restricted sense, the thought of ground is linked to the categories of the Same and the Similar.

It is indeed the ruin of this thought that is expressed by Deleuzian univocity. From the viewpoint of the dynamic power of Being, there is no admissible reason for beings to resemble anything more essential than themselves. They are an immanent production of the One, and not at all images governed by similarity. They are fortuitous modalities of the univocal and, being as far removed as possible from any mimetic hierarchy, can only be thought in their anarchic coexistence through disjunctive synthesis: "The simulacrum is not a degraded copy. It harbors a positive power which denies *the original and the copy, the model and the reproduction*" (ibid., p. 262).

And we can equally understand that Deleuze—so completely disinclined to the morose and pathetic declarations that usually accompany assertions as to the loss of any ground, so resolutely refractory to the vision of the contemporary world as one where reigns errancy, the height of distress, and the opacity of destiny—should hail with a great Nietzschean laugh the revenge of the simulacrum, the equal divergent distribution of fictions, and the overturning of icons. This is a trait of Deleuze that I particularly appreciate: a sort of unwavering love for the world as it is, a love that, beyond optimism and pessimism alike, signifies that it is always futile, always falling short of thought as such, to *judge* the world.

Of course, if we take musical order as the metaphor of the universe, as Deleuze does at the end of *The Fold*, it is clear that, today, "harmonics lose all privilege of rank (or relations, all privilege of order)" and that "divergences can be affirmed, in series that escape the diatonic scale where all tonality dissolves" (*The Fold*, p. 137). We can state that contemporary music is nongrounded because Stock-hausen, for example, identifies "variation and trajectory" (ibid.). Which means that our world, contrary to the ultimate principle of Leibniz, cannot be represented as Harmony, but is literally a world where series that in Leibniz's eyes would be in-compossible coexist in disjunctive synthesis. And it is this that we should joyously acclaim: not at all because divergence is in itself "superior" to convergence, or disso-nance to harmony — which would simply be a surreptitious return to judgment and a transcendental norm — but because *this* is the world that is ours and thought is al-ways an (ascetic, difficult) egalitarian affirmation of what is.

Rethinking a Notion of Ground

But is the restricted version of the ground given by Deleuze sufficient? Is it really so important, all this business of the model and the copy, of the Same and the Simi-lar, all this makeshift Platonism? Is it even really Platonic? One should not be too quick to believe that one has finished with the ground, or that one has succeeded in "overturning" Plato. The same, moreover, goes for Hegel, whose overturning by Marx has much rather functioned in philosophy as the underpinning for a long perpetua-tion of Hegelianism.

The term "ground" can legitimately be given to that which is determined as the real basis of singular beings, to that revealing the difference of beings to be purely formal in respect of a univocal determination of their being. Moreover, it is in the same perspective that a vigilant reading of Plato should be conducted (the Idea as that "in" a being which *exposes* it to being thought in its be-ing), rather than turning toward pictorial metaphors of the ideal model and its em-pirical imitation. The ground is, in other words, that eternal "share" of beings by which their variability and their equivocity are moored in the absolute unity of Be-ing. In this sense, not only is Deleuze's philosophy to be understood as a thinking of ground, but it is, of all the contemporary configurations, the one that most obstinately reaffirms that the thought of the multiple demands that Being be rigorously deter-mined as One. To put it another way, we can state that Deleuze's philosophy, like my own, moreover, is resolutely *classical*. And, in this context, classicism is relatively easy to define. Namely: may be qualified as classical any philosophy that does not submit to the critical injunctions of Kant. Such a philosophy considers, for all in-tents and purposes, the Kantian indictment of metaphysics as null and void, and, by way of consequence, upholds, against any "return to Kant," against the critique, moral law, and so on, that the rethinking of the univocity of ground is a necessary task for the world in which we are living today.

In this perspective, a strategic role is played in Deleuze's thought by the concept of the virtual. It is also this concept that most abruptly separates my path from his. I would readily state that, whereas my aim is to found a Platonism of the multiple, Deleuze's concern was with a Platonism of the virtual. Deleuze retains from Plato the univocal sovereignty of the One, but sacrifices the determination of the Idea as always actual. For him, the Idea is the virtual totality, the One is the infinite reservoir of dissimilar productions. *A contrario*, I uphold that the forms of the multiple are, just like the Ideas, always actual and that the virtual does not exist; I sacrifice, however, the One. The result is that Deleuze's virtual ground remains for me a transcendence, whereas for Deleuze, it is my logic of the multiple that, in not being originally referred to the act of the One, fails to hold thought firmly within immanence. In short, our contrasting forms of classicism were to prove irreconcilable.

Early in the spring of 1993, I raised the objection to Deleuze that the category of the virtual seemed to me to maintain a kind of transcendence, transposed, so to speak, "beneath" the simulacra of the world, in a sort of symmetrical relation to the "beyond" of classical transcendence. Additionally, I linked the maintaining of this inverted transcendence to the retention of the category of the All. Reaffirming the integral actuality of Being, as pure dispersion-multiple, I stated that, in my eyes, immanence excluded the All and that the only possible end point of the multiple, which is always the multiple of multiples (and never the multiple of Ones), was the multiple of nothing: the empty set.

Deleuze acknowledged at once that this issue lay at the very heart of our controversy, since, for him, insofar as the actual was composed only of *states of affairs* and *lived experience*, the plane of immanence could only be virtual and could consist only of virtualities. Insisting as always on the *reality* of the virtual, he set out its function as ground by way of three major accentuations:

1. The virtual, considered in its chaotic form, is absolute prepredicative givenness, the nonphilosophical presupposition of all philosophical thought. Just as the giving of meaning or sense proceeds from non-sense, so the consistent real, including the real-virtual, is a differentiation constructed like a section (characterized by the strictest possible proximity) through a primordial Inconsistency. The virtual here is the ground as the "there is,"[2] preceding all thought.

2. To the extent that one constructs a section of chaos (a plane of immanence), or, in other words, to the extent that one thinks *philosophically*, one extracts from all the actual (states of affairs and lived experience) that share of it that is virtual, and thought is concerned only with virtualities (that is, only virtualities populate the plane). In this way, the virtual is given a consistency and arrayed as real, in that it captures what secures beings to their being. The virtual here is the ground as the norm of the constructions that thought effects or as what guarantees that the concept fully belongs to the real.

3. To the extent that what one assigns to thought is the exploration of the simple abstract possibility and the closed reciprocal play of beings, rather than the extraction of that share of beings that is virtual, and therefore real, one still certainly constructs a plane or a consistent section of the chaotic ground. This plane, however, only "refers" beings (states of affairs and lived experience), ordering them in functions. One does not therefore go beyond the level of description: such a plane (of reference) is at best scientific (if it concerns states of affairs), at worst phenomenological (if it concerns lived experience). It does not attain the ground. This theory of the plane of reference, which is remarkable in its uniting of science and phenomenology, is a negative verification, in which Deleuze takes up the classical accusation addressed to science by metaphysics: science is "true" (Deleuze would say rather: it is a thought, a construction, a section of chaos), but it does not attain the ground of its own truth (Deleuze would say rather: it does not construct a plane of immanence, it does not realize the virtual).

For this reason, Deleuze could not understand my choosing set theory as the guide for an ontological thought of the pure multiple. As atemporal actualities, without any opening onto the virtual, sets were, for him, numbers and fell within the province of the state of affairs, science, and simple reference. Plead as I might that every figure of the type "fold," "interval," "enlacement," "serration," "fractal," or even "chaos" had a corresponding schema in a certain family of sets and was even exceeded, when thought of as a particular case of an immense spread of set configurations exhausting its multiple meaning, my pleas were to no avail. This projection of our controversy concerning the ground (the multiple-actual versus the One-virtual) onto the couple "sets/multiplicities" had no chance of resulting in a synthesis. In acknowledging this fact, Deleuze spoke highly of what he characterized as my poetic and impassioned song in praise of sets but remained steadfast on the issue on which our exchange had come to an impasse: for me, multiplicities "were" sets, for him, they "were not."

The Song of the Virtual

The Deleuzian song of the virtual is no less impassioned and certainly more poetic—it should be listened to attentively. We propose to let it resonate here, in five variations, in allowing ourselves to introduce *in fine* a number of dissonances.

1. The virtual is the very Being of beings, or we can even say that it is beings qua Being, for beings are but modalities of the One, and the One *is* the living production of its modes. The virtual must therefore never be confused with the possible; indeed, for Deleuze, this is the "only danger" (*Difference and Repetition*, p. 211; *see the selection of texts* [Appendix: "The Virtual"]). In referring a thing to its possibility, we simply separate its existence from its concept. Its concept possesses the totality of the thing's characteristics and, examining the concept, we can state that the thing is possible, which means that it can exist, it only lacks existence. But if existence is all that is lacking, if all the rest is determined as possible in the concept, then existence is "a brute eruption, a pure act or leap" (ibid.). Such a conception of existence is pure anathema for Deleuze. Existence is never a brute eruption, or a leap, because this would require that possible being and real being constitute two distinct senses of Being. But this is excluded by univocity. To exist is to come to pass on the surface of the One as a simulacrum and inflection of intensity. What results is that the One can indeed be, *in* what exists, the virtual of which the existent is an actualization or a differentiation, and that under no circumstances whatsoever can it be separated from the existent in the way that the possible is from the real. In actual fact, the so-called possible is never anything other than an image that one has fabricated of the real and that has, so to speak, been anteposed in an unassignable form of Being. It is a play of mirrors: "the possible . . . is understood as an image of the real, while the real is supposed to resemble the possible" (ibid., p. 212). For Deleuze, the possible is a category of Platonism, for which what exists has to resemble a concept that has, itself, in fact been "retroactively fabricated in the image of what resembles it" (ibid.). The virtual is, on the contrary, actualized in beings as an immanent power, and eludes any resemblance to its actualizations. "The

actualization of the virtual . . . always takes place by difference, divergence or differ-enciation. Actualization breaks with resemblance as a process no less than it does with identity as a principle. Actual terms never resemble the virtuality they actual-ize" (ibid.; translation modified).[3]

It is at this point that the song of the virtual assumes its most in-tense accents. For if, contrary to the equivocal abstraction of the possible, the virtual is the deployment of the One in its immanent differentiation, then every actualiza-tion must be understood as an innovation and as attesting to the infinite power of the One to differentiate itself on its own surface. And this power is what *sense* is, namely, the senseless act of the donation of sense: "Hence, actualization or differ-enciation is always a genuine creation" (ibid.; translation modified). That existence never has to be possible simply because it *is*, means equally that, considered in terms of the virtuality that it actualizes, the existent is, as such, not a creature but a creation.

2. The possible is opposed to the real, and immediately involves thought in the equivocal and analogy. The virtual, on the other hand, is absolutely real. Above all, we must not represent it as a latent double or ghostly prefiguration of the real. It is characterized by the process of actualization: the virtual *is* this process. Yet, thought does, of course, require the formal distinction or nominal opposition of the virtual and the actual to support the double movement of the intuition (con-sisting in thinking the actual as the actualization of the virtual, on the one hand, and the virtual as the process of production of the actual, on the other). We may therefore state that the virtual is (formally) opposed to the actual, as long as we re-member that both are real—the former as the dynamic agency of the One, the lat-ter as simulacrum. Ultimately, what counts is the divergent process of actualization by which the real is arrayed within itself as the intermingling of virtualities invested, in differing degrees of power, in the beings that they actualize.

That the virtual is real—and indeed, that face of the real which is the One—amounts consequently to thinking the specific manner in which the One, as the pure power of occurrence of its simulacra, is never given in its totality. This is impossible, because its real consists precisely in the perpetual actualizing of new virtualities. So the affirmation that the virtual is real becomes, in its turn—with Deleuze writing here under the influence of Bergson—a hymn to creation: "if the whole is not giveable, it is because it is the Open, and because its nature is to change constantly, or to give rise to something new, in short, to endure. 'The duration of the universe must therefore be one with the latitude of creation which can find place in it'" (*Cinema 1*, p. 9; quoting Bergson, *Creative Evolution*, trans. Arthur Mitchell [1954] p. 359).

3. It would be just as wrong to conceive of the virtual as a kind of indetermination, as a formless reservoir of possibilities that only actual beings identify. For were the virtual of this order, Being would have to be thought according to both the sense of its indetermination and the sense of its determination. The couple virtual/actual would start to resemble the Aristotelian couple of matter and form. In other words, "virtual" would become a category while Being, in being said in at least two senses, would no longer be univocal. It is therefore necessary to think of the virtual as "completely determined" (*Difference and Repetition*, p. 209). What does this mean? Deleuze's favorite comparison, to make us understand that the virtual is just as determined as the actual, is with mathematics. A mathematical problem is perfectly determined, just as is its solution. As regards a singular being, we can say that it is actual qua the solution of a problem borne by the virtuality that it actualizes. Virtualities, like problems, are perfectly differentiated and determined, and are just as real as actual beings, in the same way that problems are just as real as solutions. And finally, the actual bears absolutely no resemblance to the virtual, just as the solution bears no resemblance to the problem. The virtual can be said to be the locus of problems for which the actual proposes solutions.

The biological cases are isomorphic to the mathematical ones: a determined organism is both a differentiation of inorganic life qua a creative élan, and borne by a problem to be resolved, as by its own virtuality: "An organism is nothing if not the solution to a problem, as are each of its differenciated organs, such as the eye which solves a light 'problem'" (ibid., p. 211). Every creation is also a solution.

We are therefore to understand that the virtual is a ground as a function of a double determination. For while it is determined as a problem, or as the virtuality of an invented solution, it is equally determined by the circulation in the virtual of the multiplicity of problems, or seeds of actualization, because every virtuality interferes with the others, just as a problem is only constituted as a problematic locus in the proximity of other problems. A problem (a virtuality) is determined as the differentiation of another problem (of another virtuality). It follows that the sovereignty of the One is double. On the one hand, the being of the actual is a transitory modality of the One, which is thought as virtuality. On the other, the Being-One of the problems or virtualities is the virtual as the real of the problematic in general, as the universal power of problems and their solutions. The virtual is the ground for the actual, qua the being of the virtuality that the actual actualizes. But the virtual is also the ground for itself, for it is the being of virtualities, insofar as it differentiates, or problematizes, them. This is what Deleuze calls the logic of the double circuit: "Memories, dreams, even worlds are only apparent relative circuits which depend on the variations of this Whole. They are degrees or modes of actualization which are spread out between these two extremes of the actual and the virtual: the actual and *its* virtual on the small circuit, expanding virtualities in the deep circuits" (*Cinema 2*, p. 81).

We can observe that, as is almost always the case in foundational theories, it is impossible to avoid here the metaphor of depth. In addition to the determination of the virtual that has to do with the surface or the "small circuit," and which is correlated to the actual (the differentiated simulacra, or beings), there is a "deep" determination that concerns the expansion and differentiation of the virtualities themselves, and which thus forms, despite everything, a sort of interior of the One (or of the Whole). Certainly, the ground as such is the intuitive unity of both of these — namely, the thinking of the virtual as, simultaneously, virtuality of the actual and multiform expansion of the One. However, this intuitive determination is never attained without an enormous effort, and requires a certain *speed* of thought. As for the writing in which this intuition is reconcatenated, this may be seen to bear certain similarities with Deleuze's description of Foucault's discursive formations as languages that, "far from being a universal *logos*, are transient languages, capable of promoting and sometimes even of expressing mutations" (*Foucault*, p. 13; translation modified).

4. As the ground of the object, the virtual must not be thought apart from the object itself. If the being of the actual is actualization, and if actualization is the process of the virtual, then the — somewhat strange — consequence that imposes itself is as follows: "the virtual must be defined as strictly a part of the real object — as though the object had one part of itself in the virtual into which it plunged as though into an objective dimension" (*Difference and Repetition*, p. 209). And indeed, were we to separate the virtual from the actual object, univocity would be ruined, for Being would be said according to the division of the objective actual and the nonobjective virtual.

However, this doctrine concerning the object's parts is not straightforward. Deleuze himself poses the question: "How...can we speak simultaneously of both complete determination and only a part of the object?" (ibid.). In my opinion, the answer he gives is far from satisfactory and it is here that I see the stumbling block for the theory of the virtual. This answer stipulates that "Every object is double without it being the case that the two halves resemble one another, one being a virtual image and the other an actual image. They are unequal odd halves" (ibid., pp. 209–10). We can see clearly how Deleuze takes advantage here of the fact that every object, or every being, is a mere simulacrum; for this allows the timely injection of an immanent theory of the double, backed up by an optical metaphor (the possible double status of images). But it is extremely difficult to understand how the virtual can be ranked as an image, for this would seem to be the status proper to the actual, whereas it is impossible for the virtual, as the power proper to the One, to be a simulacrum. Doubtlessly, the virtual can give rise to images, but in no way can an image be given of it, nor can it itself be an image. The optical metaphor does not hold up. Certainly, it would be more fitting to say that an actual being is a "virtual image," designating in this way its two dimensions, but in that case it would be impossible to distribute the actual and the virtual as *parts* of the object.

It was exactly to avoid falling into this kind of predicament that, personally, I have posed the univocity of the actual as a pure multiple, sacrificing both the One and images. For Deleuze exemplarily demonstrates that the most magnificent contemporary attempt to restore the power of the One is at the price — as regards the thought of the actual object, inevitably determined as an image — of a very precarious theory of the Double.

5. In attempting to think through to the very end, without sacrificing the rights of the One, the virtual as a part of the real object, and therefore the image-being as divided into an actual and a virtual part, Deleuze undertakes an analytic of the indiscernible. In this he is guided, as in all the nodal points of his system, by Bergson, and particularly by the famous thesis on the surging forth of time, which "splits in two dissymmetrical jets, one of which makes all the present pass on, while the other preserves all the past" (*Cinema 2*, p. 81). We can easily recognize the actual in the passing of the present, and the virtual (or the One, or Being) in the integral preservation of the past. And indeed, it is "the actual image of the present which passes and the virtual image of the past which is preserved" (ibid.). The real object is therefore exactly like time: it is a splitting or a duplicity. We can say that the image-object *is* time, which is to say, once again, that it is a continuous creation that is, however, only effective in its division.

Yet this splitting remains enigmatic if we refer it to the pure and simple expressivity of the One. Does this not lead to the conclusion that Being is said according to the present (as a closed actuality) and according to the past (as total virtuality)? This is indeed the entire problem that is posed for Bergson, for whom the creative power of life, which is the name of the One, incessantly engenders doubles concerning which it is never certain that they are not ultimately categories or equivocal divisions of Being: matter and memory, time as duration and spatialized time, intuition and concept, evolution and species, the line of evolution that leads to bees and that which leads to man, a closed morality and an open morality, and so on. Without counting the fact that, by constantly defining becoming by splitting, one ends up closer to Hegel than one would have wished.

To conjure the double specter of equivocity and the dialectic, Deleuze ends up by posing that the two parts of the object, the virtual and the actual, cannot in fact be thought of as separate. No mark or criterion exists by which to distinguish them. They are "distinct and yet indiscernible, and all the more indiscernible because distinct, because we do not know which is one and which is the other. This is unequal exchange, or the point of indiscernibility, the mutual image" (ibid.). Ultimately, the price paid for the virtual as ground is that an object is "the point of indiscernibility of the two distinct images, the actual and the virtual" (ibid., p. 82).

We can therefore state that the complete determination of the ground as virtual implies *an essential indetermination of that for which it serves as a ground*. For any intuitive determination is necessarily disoriented when, regarding the two parts of the object, "we do not know which is one and which is the other."

This heroic effort therefore seems to me incapable of succeeding. Even when successively thought of as distinct from the possible, absolutely real, completely determined and as a strict part of the actual object, the virtual cannot, qua ground, accord with the univocity of the Being-One. The more Deleuze attempts to wrest the virtual from irreality, indetermination, and nonobjectivity, the more irreal, indetermined, and finally nonobjective the actual (or beings) becomes, because it phantasmically splits into two. In this circuit of thought, it is the Two and not the One that is instated. And when the only way of saving—despite everything—the One, is by resorting to an unthinkable Two, an indiscernibility beyond remedy, and the use of the reconciling and obscure metaphor of the "mutual image," one says to oneself that, most decidedly, the virtual is no better than the finality of which it is the inversion (it determines the destiny of everything, instead of being that to which everything is destined).[4] Let us be particularly harsh and invoke Spinoza against his major, and indeed sole, truly modern disciple: just like finality, the virtual is *ignorantiae asylum*.[5]

I must therefore return, as is the law in philosophy—that discipline of thought in which discussion is at once omnipresent and without any other effect than internal—to my own song: the One is not, there are only actual multiplicities, and the ground is void.

F I V E

Time and Truth

I HAVE already had the opportunity to mention that Deleuze's philosophy, like my own, is classical in nature (a metaphysics of Being and of the ground). In my case, the classical consequence of this classicism is that the idea of truth is central. Indeed, most of *L'Etre et l'événement*[1] is devoted to the construction of this idea, which is rendered extremely complex by the conditions of our epoch. In these circumstances, it is natural to ask what becomes of truth in Deleuze's work—and, in particular, whether the fact that beings are simulacra and that they therefore manifest, in the Nietzschean tradition, "the highest power of the false" (*The Logic of Sense*, p. 263) prevents the virtual as ground from acting to secure a possible intuitive truth.

Certainly, Deleuze would readily remark with disapprobation the foregrounding of the question of truth by a philosophy. He wrote to me that he had never felt either the need or the taste for such a notion. He stated that truth, for him, was merely the relation of a transcendent with its attendant functions, that it concerned the *possibility of an actual*, whereas the *reality of a virtual* is something completely different from truth. Truths are necessarily analogical or equivocal, whereas concepts are absolutely univocal.

There would seem, therefore, little room for doubt. At best, the idea of truth is ascribed by Deleuze to science alone (the plane of reference), because it requires:

- a point of transcendence (which contravenes univocity because of the equation immanence = univocity, which one could rewrite as multiplicities = One);

- the referring of actual beings, not to the real virtuality that founds them, but to the play of mirrors that characterizes the possible;

- analogical circuits, that presuppose the use of categories entailing the division of Being.

We can, moreover, fairly well sum up this judgment by saying that, for Deleuze, truth is a category, and even the category of categories or *the* Category: it is normative (it requires the transcendence of judgment), analogical (it is said equivocally of all the forms of Being), abstract (it verifies a possibility instead of actualizing a virtuality), and mediatory (the objective it sets for becoming is the internalization of its being, which is the assumption of its truth). One understands why Deleuze could declare never having had "any taste" for the category of truth, which, in the terms of his logic, is a much harsher condemnation than if he had pronounced its inconsistency: "taste" signals, in fact, as an affect, the setting into motion of an intuition. And we have just indicated why intuition, as the double trajectory of power, has nothing to do with evaluations based on the criterion of the true.

The Power of the False

But we must ask the same question concerning truth as we did concerning the ground: is not Deleuze's explicit conception of this notion remarkably limited? Does it not depend on the pared-down version of "Platonism" that Deleuze concocts for the purpose in hand? When he strikes up the joyful song hailing the ascent of the multiple simulacra (which we have shown to be, perhaps rather less joyfully, the triumph of the One), Deleuze employs a very beautiful image that subverts the *Odyssey*—namely, that of the "triumph of the false pretender" (ibid., p. 262). But he immediately adds that "the false pretender cannot be called false in relation to a presupposed model of truth" (ibid., pp. 262–63). The triumph is that of "the effect of the functioning of the simulacrum as machinery—a Dionysian machine" (ibid., p. 263).

That this machinic effect ruins the hierarchical arrangement of the paradigm and its imitation can be accorded without any difficulty. But is "truth" spoken of only in the sense of that which judges the mimetic appearances and reestablishes the rights of the real essence? We can quite happily grant that "[b]y rising to the surface, the simulacrum makes the Same and the Similar, the model and the copy, fall under the power of the false (phantasm)" (ibid.). However, it nonetheless remains the case that, in this affair, "false" refers uniquely to a category of truth precisely founded on the Same of the model and the Similar of the copy—a category concerning which I do not believe it is an exaggeration to claim that it has never been advanced by any philosopher other than as a mediatory image that the philosopher's entire thought will subsequently be devoted to dismantling. This is especially the case for Plato, who, for example, consecrates the beginning of the *Parmenides* to establishing the inanity of this image, which he abundantly uses elsewhere.

Thus the question still remains unresolved as to whether Deleuze's very understandable "lack of taste" for the analogical conception of truth ("the true" as the share of actual being that is analogical to its being, or as the faithful copy of its Idea) might not indicate some profound, and more secret, taste for *another* idea of truth. Indeed, this other idea of truth, I would suggest, is one that Deleuze, with the violent courtesy that I discern in his style and thought, was to implacably defend: an idea that is all the more devious for giving to truth the name of the false— the *power* of the false—and for the fact that the process of this truth is no longer judgment, but (in conformity with the requisites of the intuition, which, as we have seen, is always a looped trajectory) a sort of *narration*.

We should be sensitive to the nuance of cruel certainty in the following passage from *Cinema 2*, in which the case of Borges serves as the starting point for thought's experimentation, for it is here that we can discern, in my opinion, the occurrence of an idea of truth specific to Deleuze:

> narration ceases to be truthful, that is, to claim to be true, and becomes fundamentally falsifying. This is not at all a case of 'each has its own truth', a variability of content. It is a power of the false which replaces and supersedes the form of the true, because it poses the simultaneity of incompossible presents, or the coexistence of not-necessarily true pasts. . . . Falsifying narration . . . poses inexplicable differences in the present and alternatives which are undecidable between true and false in the past. The truthful man dies, every model of truth collapses, in favour of the new narration. (*Cinema 2*, p. 131; translation modified)

This text gives rise to five remarks:

1. "Truth" is absolutely still formulated therein in terms of the restricted version of the model (and the copy). The death of the "truthful man"

never means anything other than the death of the Nietzschean construction named "Platonism."

2. The posing of undecidable alternatives between the true and the false (to avoid confusion, it would be better to say between the veridical and the erroneous) has always been constitutive of the movement of truth. Plato is exemplary in this respect: not only does he view the true as having necessarily to pass through aporia, but he does not hesitate to start entire texts with an *absolute* undecidability (for example, that it is both possible *and* impossible to teach virtue, or that it is false both that the One is *and* that it is not).

3. The theme of narration as the flexible and paradoxical vector of truth is as old as philosophy itself. The tales of Achilles and his tortoise, the anecdotes about the quarrel of contingent futures (to which Deleuze himself, quite rightly, attaches the greatest importance), the vindications that flawlessly demonstrate, first, that Helen is magnificent, and then that Helen is ignoble, did not await the (inspired) work of Borges, nor the "new narration," to delight in putting every theory of truth to the test. Here, once again, Plato proves to be a master. Who could maintain that the myth of Er the Pamphylian, at the end of the *Republic*, is a transparent narrative? It consists entirely of traps and bifurcations.

I would add that, personally, I have always conceived truth as a random course or as a kind of escapade, posterior to the event and free of any external law, such that the resources of narration are required *simultaneously* with those of mathematization for its comprehension. There is a constant circulation from fiction to argument, from image to formula, from poem to matheme — as indeed the work of Borges strikingly illustrates.

It is quite possible therefore that the processes of the "power of the false" are strictly indiscernible from the repertoire composed by the processes of the power of the true.

4. A simple explanation can be found for this indiscernibility.

For those who think, like myself, that the univocity of Being requires its integral *actuality*, the theme of truth is necessarily given as the immanent — and equally actual — inscription of that share of being that founds beings (the Idea for Plato, the negative for Hegel, the generic in my own conceptual undertaking . . .). The difficulty here — which can only be dealt with by the resources of aporia, the twists of narration, and sophisticated argument — consists in constructively locating the *actual forms* of Being-true, for they cannot be referred to any virtuality. Let us say that the protocol involved is that of the *formal isolation* of truths in the infinite deployment of actual beings.

On the other hand, for those for whom the univocity of Being requires that it be essentially *virtual*, the theme of truth is necessarily given as *power*. From the viewpoint of this power, the actual forms of beings can indeed be considered as simulacra, or anarchic agencies of the false. For truth is coextensive with the productive capacity of the One-virtual, and does not reside as such in any particular actual outcome, in isolation from the rest. Accordingly, the difficulty in this instance is no longer that of isolating forms-of-the-true[2] in the actual, but of linking the anarchy of the simulacra to an immanent affirmation-of-the-true. However, this affirmation exists nowhere else than in its actualizations and the power is really the power *of the false*. The task is thus to circulate in the cases and the forms of the false in such a way that, under their constraint and in being exposed ascetically to their Dionysian machinery, we are transfixed by the intuitive trajectory that effects the unification of the "descent" toward the One-true and the "reascent" toward the Multiple-false. This is the intuition of power as such. The problem posed here — which requires, no less than the problem concerning the isolation of the actual forms of the true, that we draw upon everything, from hymns to algorithms, that can be put to account — is that of a *true virtual totalization of the actual forms of the false*. But it is still and always the question of truth that is involved.

Deleuze praises "Nietzsche, who, under the name of 'will to power', substitutes the power of the false for the form of the true, and resolves the crisis of truth, wanting to settle it once and for all, but, in opposition to Leibniz, in favour of the false and its artistic, creative power" (*Cinema 2*, p. 131). The objection can be raised against Deleuze here that the operation he describes is tautological. If you think the true as (virtual) power, and not as (actual) form, then it is certain that the forms of the true will be the false-product of this power. Conversely, if you think the true as (actual) form, then (virtual) power will be the false-form par excellence, the *generic* form of inactuality.

All in all, "power of the false" is exactly the Deleuzian name, borrowed from Nietzsche, for truth.

5. One can observe that this passage on the power of the false gives an extreme importance to the question of time. What Borges is credited with, what enables him to "supersede the form of the true," entails narrative manipulations of the present and the past: accordingly, we find the coexistence of pasts whose truth or falseness is doubtful, even though they are supposed to have taken place, and the simultaneity of presents that should exclude one another. It would appear that, for Deleuze, truth (the power of the false) and time belong to the same register of thought. And this is, in fact, the case: the "royal road" of Deleuze's idea of the true is his theory of time.

Primacy of Time and Detemporalization

The connection between truth and time first takes a negative form: "If we take the history of thought, we see that time has always put the notion of truth into crisis" (ibid., p. 130; *see the selection of texts* [Appendix: "Time versus Truth"]). In support of this thesis, Deleuze draws on (as we have already hinted) that important *topos* of Greek philosophy, the paradox of contingent futures. The matrix of this paradox can be summed up as follows. Let us suppose that it is true to state that "the event x may take place tomorrow." This amounts to maintaining, in the present, that x may not take place (for if not, what would be true would be that x *must* take place). The result of this is that, if x does take place tomorrow, this true thought (x may not take place) will be rendered false, in such a way that we have to relinquish the idea that the past, as that having-taken-place, is always true. Similarly, the impossible (that x does not take place — which is impossible once x has taken place) turns out to have been as though engendered by its own "true" possibility (the thought that it is possible that x not take place).

If we ask ourselves what specific use Deleuze makes of this "paradox," we find that it is to show that there can be no straightforward connection between truth and the form of time. And this is why philosophy has seen itself condemned, for such a long time, to "keep the true away from the existent, in the eternal or in what imitates the eternal" (ibid.). The theory of the power of the false lifts this condemnation: primacy is given to time, while truth has to be deposed.

It should be noted that this conclusion is never anything other than a choice. For, the fact that the relation between truth and time is fraught with very real difficulties can lead us to conclude, without viewing this as a "condemnation," that it is the category of time that is contradictory and empirical, and that it is legitimate, and indeed joyous, to suppress it in favor of truths. This is, in fact, what I think: truths are actual multiplicities with a much higher "Dionysian" value than that accruing to any sort of phenomenological salvaging of time. I would readily go so far as to say that the backdrop to this value has always been the conviction that the actuality of truths (be these, for instance, scientific, political, amorous, or artistic) is transtemporal — that we *really* are the contemporaries of Archimedes and Newton, Spartacus and Saint-Just, Dame Murasaki and Héloïse, Phidias and Tintoretto. Which means that we think with — and in — them, without the least need of a temporal synthesis.

On the face of it, Deleuze maintains the contrary. He prefers time to truth, and all the more insofar as "the only subjectivity is time, non-chronological time grasped in its foundation" (ibid., p. 82). On the face of it. For we need to be attentive to the strange determinations of time — "non-chronological," "grasped in its foundation" — in the formulation above. The problem is made more complicated by the fact that, for Deleuze, as we shall show:

- time *is* truth itself;

- as truth, time is not temporal: it is integral virtuality; and

- the absolute being of the past is indiscernible from eternity.

The result is that it is not exaggerated to state that the classicism of Deleuze attains its final form when *the temporal power of the false* is thought, according to an essential and particularly difficult intuition, *as one and same thing as the eternity of the true*. And this is an eternity of which the mode of being is (eternal) return.

This statement once again makes Deleuze an involuntary Platonist. We know the master's formula: time is the "moving image of eternity."[3] One might at first believe that it condenses everything that Deleuze renounces: the reduction of sensible time — concrete time — to the miserable state of a copy of an eternal model. But if the image is referred, as it should be, to its specific being as simulacrum (and not to *mimesis*), and eternity to the One qua integral virtual, we can understand that, for Deleuze as well, for Deleuze above all, the essence of time consists in expressing the eternal. As Deleuze forcefully puts it, the time-images, which can be situated in the creative power of the All, are "volume-images which are beyond movement itself" (*Cinema 1*, p. 11). This clearly underlines that the profound being of time, its truth, is immobile.

But how are we to think this immobile totalization that founds the mobility of time? Deleuze once again positions himself in Bergson's wake, with the crucial intuition that he follows here linking together two ideas.

On the one hand, the past "is constituted not after the present that it was but at the same time" (*Cinema 2*, p. 81). This point strictly conforms to the logic of the One. Were the past only an aftermath of the present, it would not be creation or power, but irremediable absence; it would be the production of the nothingness of the present-that-passes. Being would then have to be said, at the same point, in two different senses: according to its mobile-being and according to its absence. There would be a *nostalgic* division of Being. Nothing is more foreign to Deleuze (or to Bergson) than this nostalgia. The past is a positive production of time. Far from being characterized by a loss of being or an annihilation of the precariousness of becoming, it is an enhancement or supplement of being, an incorporation into the changing of the One (but the One is its own changing). The present is, in fact, a point where the One opens up (but the One is the Open), and there is an intermingling of a variation of the One (of pure duration) and a superficial mobility. It is here, at this point, that time splits, taking the aspect of a *double creation*. Time is creative splitting: "time . . . has to split the present in two heterogeneous directions, one of which is launched towards the future while the other falls into the past" (ibid.). Such splitting is the *operation* of time as a configuration of the power of the One. For every occurrence of a simulacrum's coming-to-the-surface (which is nothing other than actualization qua a present "which is launched towards the future") must, in its pure being, be an immanent change of the One (the creative incorporation of the past, its *virtualization*).

On the other hand, the past that is created in this way is incorporated into an enormous total "memory," which is the being of time as pure duration—that permanent qualitative change where all the past is operative, just like all the virtual. Moreover, the correspondences are strict. Just as every actual being has its own virtuality within itself, so within every present lies its own past. And just as the different virtualities are differentiated "in depth," with these differentiations constituting the virtual, so the different pasts agglomerate and combine together to constitute the duration, or total past. In each case, there is "a small internal circuit between a present and *its own* past" and "deeper and deeper circuits which are themselves virtual, which each time mobilize the whole of the past, but in which the relative circuits bathe or plunge to trace an actual shape and bring in their provisional harvest" (ibid., p. 80).

We can note in this choice of image—the "provisional" harvest—an emergent opposition between the transient mobility of the actual dimension of the present and the latent eternity of the incorporation of its virtual dimension within "the whole of the past."

Pure duration, the great total past that is one with the virtual, cannot be qualified as temporal because it is the being of time, its univocal designation according to the One. The different determinations of time are "sections" of this duration—with the word "section" always conveying, in Deleuze's texts, a complete intuition of actualization (philosophy itself, considered as the construction of a plane of immanence, is a section of chaos). Deleuze was to elucidate Bergson (or Bergson was to elucidate Deleuze, in conformity with the active existence of the past within, or copresent with, the present) by distinguishing, respectively: immobile, or instantaneous, sections, that are objects; mobile sections, that are movements; and finally, total sections or planes — the ground of the other sections — where it is really a matter of the intemporal One, and where "objects, by gaining depth, by losing their contours, are united in duration" (*Cinema 1*, p. 11).

One will remark here the stylistic economy characterizing the ground that always undoes what it founds: it is by relinquishing their form and becoming dissolved in their own (virtual) depth, that beings (objects) are at last arrayed, thought, and given an image according to the univocity of the One. As in every great classical conception, *truth is the undoing, or defection, of the object of which it is the truth*.

Deleuze's intuition culminates in the complete determination of the whole (or the One) — qua the founding intemporality of time — as Relation. Nothing shows more clearly that, if time is truth, then the being of time, as the being of truth, has to be able to be thought under a concept from which all temporal dimension has been eliminated.

Why is it the case that "if one had to define the whole, it would be defined as Relation?" (ibid., p. 10). Let us follow here the thread of the analysis of time. An object is never anything else than an immobile section of duration or instantaneous dimension of the present. It cannot therefore, *in itself*, bear a relation to other objects because no pure present can communicate directly with any other. Presents are simple, transient coexistences. Inasmuch as there are temporal relations, or something like time *as such*, it can only be in depth, in the differentiations that take place between singular pasts in the total Past, in the "large circuit" of virtualities. But these deep differentiations are nothing other than qualitative changes of the whole, or the being of the One as change. The result is, negatively, that "Relation is not a property of objects" and, positively, that "[r]elations . . . belong to . . . the whole" (ibid.). Movement in the space of objects is, as actuality or simulacrum, the unbound contiguity of presents-objects. But, in its virtual depth, in its truth, it is the internal change of the One, which is expressed on the surface by temporal relations, such as the Simultaneous, the Antecedent, Memory, Project, and so on — relations that are unintelligible as long as one imagines that they are properties of the instantaneous dimension of the present. "By movement in space, the objects of a set change their respective positions. But, through relations, the whole is transformed or changes qualitatively" (ibid.).

It is therefore possible to conclude that "We can say of duration itself or of time, that it is the whole of relations" (ibid.). It is this "whole" of relations that Deleuze names—in employing the oh so very Platonic capitalization!—"the Relation." And it is in this way that the intuition that leads from time as the site of truth to the detemporalization of time comes to completion.

Memory and Forgetting

We can observe that this proximity to Plato is equally a proximity to Hegel. If time (as virtual, or integral, past) is the Relation, then surely we are not so very far from the famous formula "Time is the being-there of the Concept."[4] For Hegel also arrays the intelligibility of beings under the law of the becoming of the One, which is, at the same time, the One as becoming; and this means that he, too, has both to render full justice to time and, ultimately, to detemporalize it in the circular immanence of the absolute Idea. The quarrel between Deleuze and Hegel bears on the nature of the operations involved (the negative versus the expressive, the dialectic versus intuition, the vertical deployment versus the "crowned anarchy"), not on the global framework.

For this reason, it has always seemed to me that a part of my dispute with Hegel also held good for Deleuze.

Time is for me a category derived from presentation as such,[5] and it is in itself multiple. I would state that time (or rather *a* time—that of the situation)[6] is the being-*not-there* of the concept. A truth is always the undoing of a time, just as a revolution is the end of an epoch. It is therefore essential for me that truth be thought, not as time or as the intemporal being of time, but as *interruption*.

It seems to me that Deleuze and Hegel pose, on the contrary, that truth is ultimately memory, or incorporation within Being of its own actualized fecundity: absolute past. The point on which they diverge—and this is very important—is the structure of the memory: for the one, this is Relation, or virtualizations and differentiations, while, for the other, it is a question of Stages, that is, monumental and obligatory figures. However, the consequence of the sovereignty of the One is still the same: truth is the immanent preservation (as virtuality, or as concept) of what, inherent to the One, has testified to its power—as actuality, for Deleuze, as effectivity, for Hegel.

But if the "there is" is pure multiplicity, if all is actual, and if the One is not, then it is not toward Memory that one should turn to search for the true. On the contrary, truth is forgetful, it is even, contrary to what Heidegger thinks, the forgetting of forgetting, the radical interruption, caught up in the sequence of its effects. And this forgetting is not the simple forgetting of this or that, but the forgetting of time itself: the moment when we live as if time (*this* time) had never existed, or, in conformity with the profound maxim of Aristotle, as if we were immortal — for the common being of all time is death. This, to my mind, is the real experience of (political) revolutions, (amorous) passions, (scientific) inventions, and (artistic) creations. It is in this abolition of time that is engendered the eternity of truths.

It is in his *Foucault* that the most appeased texts on truth written by Deleuze are to be found. Here, beyond the Nietzschean imprecations against Platonism and the apologia of the *Pseudos*, Deleuze fully admits — or Foucault makes Deleuze admit — that there exist games of truth, that truth "is inseparable from the procedure establishing it" (*Foucault*, p. 63). He identifies this procedure with the disjunctive synthesis, which is undeniably admissible given that this synthesis — the ascetic experience of the nonrelation — is the obligatory point of departure for the entire intuitive trajectory that leads to truth as Relation: "Truth is defined neither by conformity or common form, nor by a correspondence between the two forms [Deleuze is speaking here of Foucault, thus the "two forms" are the visible and language]. There is a disjunction between speaking and seeing" (ibid., p. 64). But the procedure of truth, in the form that Deleuze deciphers it in Foucault, ultimately results in memory, and indeed even "'absolute memory' or memory of the outside, beyond the brief memory inscribed in strata and archives" (ibid., p. 107). The advent of truth occurs when time becomes a subject, in the sense that there takes place the intuition of duration: the plunging into the deep strata of the virtual, or the long, enduring memory's immersion within the integral past as the permanent action of the One. The becoming-truth of the subject, qua the becoming-subject of time, is what "forces every present into forgetting, but preserves the whole of the past within memory" (ibid., p. 108). And if forgetting bars the possibility of ever returning to what precedes the present, it is memory that consequently founds the "necessity of recommencing" (ibid.; translation modified).

Truth, which begins as disjunctive synthesis, or the experience of the separation of the present, culminates in the memorial injunction to recommence perpetually.

This amounts to saying that there is no commencement, but only an abolished present (undergoing virtualization) and a memory that rises to the surface (undergoing actualization).

And this is what I cannot consent to — for I maintain that every truth is the end of memory, the unfolding of a commencement.

S I X

Eternal Return and Chance

THAT TRUTH is memory can equally be expressed another way: truth only occurs by reoccurring, it is return. And that truth is not temporal, but identical to the being of time, amounts to saying that its return is eternal.

One can argue that most of Deleuze's work is devoted to defending, unfolding, and understanding ever more comprehensively the founding intuition of Nietzsche concerning the eternal return. I say this in admiration, for I believe that every truth is a fidelity.[1] Deleuze's fidelity to the eternal return was all the more necessary given the serious misinterpretations that constantly threaten this motif—misinterpretations that are, moreover, particularly dangerous if the intuition is understood in the form that its author usually couches it: the eternal return of the Same.

The Same is an old philosophical category; in Plato's *Sophist*, it is one of the five "supreme kinds of forms" that conduct (so Deleuze thinks) an equivocal division of Being. The misinterpretations that have prevented the good, Dionysian, news of the eternal return of the Same from being fully elucidated, and of which the danger was so evident that Nietzsche was led to treat his own dazzling intuition with a sort of reserve and semisilence, are all linked to the equivocities of the Same.

On Three Misinterpretations

There are at least three deformations of the motif of the eternal return, all of which make it a category or a transcendent abstraction.

1. The eternal return can be considered to be said of the One itself; with the One figuring here as a sort of subject of the eternal return. It is the One that returns, and returns eternally. But how can the One return? This is possible if the One is thought according to its identity, One = One, which is Fichte's starting point, as well as a possible way of understanding Parmenides' intuition (Being is One because selfsameness constitutes its only identity, and it is circular or sphere-like because, in accordance with this identity, it can do nothing but return). Deleuze stated that, in such a conception of the eternal return of the Same, the identity of the One is a "principle" (*Difference and Repetition*, p. 126). It follows that the One has a transcendent position in relation to the multiple, for the differences are subordinated to it, just as a diversity is to its principle. The multiple as such is only taken up within the identical return of the One and its inalterable permanence to the extent that it partakes of this in a degradative manner—as what distorts and corrupts the principle of identity. The multiple is recalled to its essential being, and the form of corrupted being that it represents is rectified and corrected by the return of the Same, by the reaffirmation that the One is the One, just as in certain religions, belief and the salvation that is attached to it are integrally contained in the proposition that God is God. And, of course, Being is equivocal. For it is said of the One as of what returns, and of the multiple as of what must not return. It is said of the identical as of what is superior to difference.

We know enough to be able to dismiss this misinterpretation concerning the Same. The One cannot return as a subject or as identity. For the One is already in itself nothing other than *the power by which its immanent modes occur.* And this occurrence cannot be specified as identity, it escapes the tautology One = One, because it is the Open, change, duration, Relation. No thought *of* the One exists that would permit its identification and its recognition when it returns. There are only thoughts *in* the One, or according to the One, and these are themselves inflections of its power, trajectories, and intuitions.

It is necessary to add that univocity precludes any idea of the return of the One. For if the One had to return, as Deleuze remarks along with Nietzsche, it would first have to become absent to itself, to come outside of itself. But how could it do this, if it is univocal? It would be necessary for it to be subject to the work of the negative within itself, as are the successive figures of the Absolute for Hegel. And Being, even if it is conceived as a dialectical *movement*, or as the principle of this movement, would then be said according to at least two senses: the coming-out-of-itself and the return, immediacy and negation, externalization and internalization.

We must therefore conclude that the eternal return (repetition) is "not the permanence of the One" (ibid.; translation modified), and that "the subject of the eternal return is not the same" (ibid.).

2. The eternal return can be considered to be not, strictly or ontologically speaking, the return of the One itself, but a sort of formal law imposed on chaos. The One-world would result from two principles, and not from one alone. On the one hand, there would be tendencies toward dissolution and corruption as immanent determinations of what there is, or of matter; and, on the other, the constraint of the cycle, of return, or of the restoration of the Same, as the legislative correction of the first tendency. The Universe would be the—perhaps transitory—outcome of a struggle of principle between dissolution and return, somewhat similar to the way that, in Empedocles' conception, Being is the stage on which is waged the conflict between Love and Hate, the principle of conjunction and the principle of dissolution. One could even attempt a "Deleuzian" interpretation of this manner of understanding the return. The reascent of the virtual would be the return, or the engagement of the One in the simulacra or beings, while the beings themselves, in their subjection to the disjunctive synthesis, would signify heterogeneity and dissolution.

But we know that, for Deleuze, there are not beings "themselves" that could be presupposed to come under an internal principle of dissolution and an external principle of repetition, or return. Certainly, every object is double—being endowed with an actual and a virtual part. Yet, it is absolutely excluded (even though, as I have stated, this exclusion is difficult to maintain) that the two parts of the object come under different principles. Inasmuch as the object's actual part is intelligible, this intelligibility consists precisely in the intuition of its virtuality. And inasmuch as its virtual part is intelligible, this consists once again in virtuality itself, but in being referred, this time, to the total play of the virtual. There is the small circuit and the large circuit of the intuition of virtualities, and it is impossible for the circuit itself to split according to different principles. The power of the One qua thought is, moreover, precisely this: there is only one intuition. Such is the profound ontological meaning that Deleuze gives to a well-known remark of Bergson, namely, that every great philosophy is nothing other than the insistence, the return, of a unique intuition.

Let me say in passing that this point should give food for thought to those who still believe that one can invoke Deleuze's name as a way of sanctioning "democratic" debates, the legitimate diversity of opinions, the consumerist satisfaction of desires, or, again, the mixture of vague hedonism and "interesting conversations" that passes for an art of living. They should examine attentively who Deleuze's heroes of thought are: Melville's Bartleby the scrivener ("I would prefer not to")[2] or Beckett's Unnamable ("you must go on, I can't go on, I'll go on").[3] They would learn in what the *discipline* of the unique intuition consists.

Deleuze rejects all the more virulently a legislative reading of the return in that it is, for him, a Platonic paradigm: "The manifest content of the eternal return can be determined in conformity to Platonism in general. It represents then the manner in which chaos is organized by the action of the demiurge, and on the model of the Idea which imposes the same and the similar on him. The eternal return, in this sense, is the becoming-mad that has been mastered, made monocentric, and determined to copy the eternal" (*The Logic of Sense*, p. 263; translation modified). The eternal return cannot be a law, forcefully applied to a rebellious matter, without becoming a transcendent principle.

Obviously, it is in no way certain that this altogether coherent conclusion needs to refer critically to "Platonism" for its legitimacy. When the demiurge in the fable of the *Timaeus* (a text that is yet again a novel, a fabulous and eccentric narration) first exercises force, it is in order to adjust the circles of the Same and of the Other, which do not "want" to have anything to do with each other. One could therefore just as well argue that the cosmic return, for Plato, is founded on a disjunctive synthesis. And would we then be so far from Deleuze, when he writes that "Only the divergent series, insofar as they are divergent, return" (ibid., p. 264)? Plato's picturesque cosmology, with its biological constructions and metaphorical mathematics, its conceptual persona (the Demiurge), and its mysterious "errant cause,"[4] its forced disjunctions, and the strange relation, neither internal nor external, that it weaves between the cosmic time of the return and eternity, has always seemed to me to have something Deleuzian about it.

But if we confine ourselves—as we should—to the "Platonism" that functions as a prop for Deleuze's intuition, then it is certain that, in "the eternal return of the Same," the return is subordinated to the Same, in the sense that what returns must be the copy of an Idea; that is, it must be the same as the Idea. Furthermore, "eternal" is not an intrinsic attribute of the return—it is not the return that is the active being, or the *creation*, of eternity—but, rather, the return is a simple material imitation of a separate eternity, and is, in itself, inactive.

We must therefore understand that, for Deleuze, the eternal return is absolutely not a principle of order imposed on chaos or matter. On the contrary, the "secret of the eternal return is that...it is nothing other than chaos itself, or the power of affirming chaos" (ibid.). What returns as living eternity is that every (actual) order is never anything else than a simulacrum and that the being that is to be reaffirmed of this simulacrum is the chaotic interference of all the virtualities in the One. It is not the One that returns, as we know already. Rather, what returns is that every type of order and every value, *thought as inflections of the One*, are only differences of differences, transitory divergences, whose profound being is the universal interference of virtualities. It is "all the [differences] insofar as they complicate their difference within the chaos which is without beginning or end" (ibid.)[5] that return. The return is the eternal affirmation of the fact that the only Same is precisely chaotic difference.

The exact position of the Same, in the expression "eternal return of the Same," then becomes clear, according to an intuitive line, tautly drawn between the peril of understanding that it is the One that returns (the return *of* the One) and that of understanding that it is the One that imposes the law of return on the diverse (a return that proceeds from the One, but outside itself). The axiom, which is extremely difficult, is as follows: "the eternal return...is the only same" (*Difference and Repetition*, p. 126). It is necessary to intuit here that *the sameness does not preexist the eternal return, as either the identity of the One or the paradigm of a relation between beings.* There is only something of the order of the "same" to the extent that absolute difference—that is, chaos as the name of the Open—is affirmed. But this affirmation is the return itself.

Neither the identity of the One, nor the external law of the multiple, the return is the *creation* of the Same for the different, and by the different. Only in this sense can one say that it is "the one *of the* multiple" (ibid.).[6] What this means is not at all that the one becomes separate from or subsumes the multiple in the return, but rather, that the multiple is affirmed in the return, beyond its consistency as a simulacrum, as both superficial disjunctive synthesis and deep chaos.

This is why Deleuze opposes to the Greek figure of the cosmos— that transcendent, legalized form of return—what he calls, in borrowing from Joyce, the *chaosmos*. And it is equally why, in joyfully affirming the simulacra that the real return grounds and dissolves, Deleuze opposes to the coherency that the return in its corrupted sense is supposed to bestow upon the appearances, a "chao-errancy."[7]

3. Finally, the return of the same can be considered to be a hidden algorithm that would govern chance, a sort of statistical regularity, as in probability theory. Short series might give the appearance of arbitrariness and divergence. One would see, for example, certain cases or certain events occur a great number of

times, while others, of comparable probability, would never, or almost never, occur — as when in the game of "head or tails," it comes up "tails" ten times in a row. But we can observe that it simply requires a sufficiently long series for these divergences to become muted, and for the law of the Same to tend to prevail between events of identical probability. For if you toss a coin ten thousand times, the number of "tails" outcomes will approach the number of "heads" outcomes, in the sense that the divergence between each of these numbers and 5,000 — the number that is the ideal realization of the Same, with exactly 5,000 outcomes for each of the two events — will be minor in comparison with the total number (10,000) of events. And if you toss an infinite number of times, then there will be an exact return of the Same, with the difference between the outcomes "tails" and "heads" tending toward zero. The return of the Same would then be that which, according to an infinite power of the play of the world, cancels chance.

Do we need to add that this return is eternal? Yes, in fact we do. For, although divergences and differences without a concept can always subsist over a measurable or finite time, the conformity of the real to its probability is necessarily affirmed beyond or at the limit of time. For an eternal player, who really tosses the coin an infinite number of times, "tails" will come up exactly as many times as "heads." It is therefore from the standpoint of eternity, or according to eternity, that the return of the same imposes its law of equilibrium on chance. We can equally state, according to this way of viewing things, that the eternal return of the Same is what affirms the nonexistence of the improbable.

Yet, if the question of chance, the game, or the dice throw is of such significance for Deleuze (as it is for Mallarmé and Nietzsche), it is because he seeks — and this is of the utmost importance to him — to *refute* the probabilistic conception of the eternal return and to maintain the rights of divergence and the improbable within the very heart of the infinite power of the One.

Let us note in passing that Deleuze's intention here is in sharp contrast to that of Mallarmé — a thinker concerning whom Deleuze, between his strongly critical remarks in *Difference and Repetition* and the attempts at annexation in *Foucault* and *The Fold*, was to change considerably his position. In my mind, Deleuze's initial attitude was the right one. Absolutely no compromise is possible between Deleuze's vitalism and Mallarmé's subtractive ontology. As regards chance, in particular, the maxims of the one and the other are diametrically opposed. The maxim of Mallarmé is: "the Infinite proceeds from Chance — that Chance you have negated." That of Deleuze, as we are about to see, must be expressed as follows: "Chance proceeds from the Infinite — that Infinite you have affirmed."

Why is it so important, in Deleuze's philosophy, that the conception of the eternal return of the Same as the suppression of chance by the infinite be considered a misinterpretation? It is because, were it correct, *the infinite power of the One would not be difference, but identity; it would not be disequilibrium of the virtual, but equilibrium of the actual.* And still more profoundly, the One would cease to be identifiable as the production of divergent simulacra, dependent on disjunctive syntheses. It would *manifest itself* as the jurisdiction of the Same, by equalizing "ad infinitum" all the chances and all the events, while canceling all the improbabilities. It would then be necessary for Being to be said in at least two senses: that of the random "casts" of events (within temporal finitude), and that of their egalitarian equivalence, or their pure and simple necessity (within the effect of the eternal return of the Same). To maintain univocity, it is therefore necessary to maintain chance, divergence, and the improbable, even under the conditions of the infinite.

But what then becomes of the eternal return—how is it aligned with chance? This is an extremely difficult question, and despite the frequency with which Deleuze, from one book to the next, readdressed it, we cannot be sure that his answer is satisfactory.

As always, Deleuze does not ignore this difficulty—he faces up to it, completely lucidly. He knows, for example, that as soon as there is a second throw of the dice, the proceedings of the Same get under way and will ineluctably win out in the infinite: "the second throw perhaps operates under conditions that are partially determined by the first, as in a Markov chain, where we have a succession of partial reconcatenations" (*Foucault*, p. 117; translation modified). He speaks of the impurity of the series of throws, which are deployed "in mixtures of chance and dependency." In short, Deleuze wants, against probability theory, both to maintain the figure of the game of chance and to withdraw it from the jurisdiction of the Same. Or, conversely, he wants to assume the motif of the eternal return, without ever sacrificing chance.

The "True Throw of the Dice"

For this, it is necessary, against empiricism and formal algorithms, to define the "true throw of the dice" (*Difference and Repetition*, p. 304). There are, all in all, three characteristics of this true dice throw.

1. It is *unique.* For were there (really, ontologically) several throws, the statistical revenge of the Same would be ineluctable. This is, no doubt, the point at which Deleuze's philosophy as philosophy of the One is at its most concentrated. For, if there is only one throw of the dice, if the "throws are formally distinct, but

with regard to an ontologically unique throw, while the outcomes implicate, displace and recover their combinations in one another throughout the unique and open space of the univocal" (ibid.), then one has to uphold that the plurality of events is purely formal, and that there is only one event, which is, as it were, the event of the One. And we have seen that Deleuze does not, in fact, draw back from this conse- quence. Being is indeed the unique event, "the unique cast for all throws" (*The Logic of Sense*, p. 180).

2. This unique cast is the *affirmation of the totality of chance*. Chance cannot, in fact, consist in a succession of throws, which would lay it open to the comparison of probabilities, and ultimately, in the infinite, to its cancellation within the equilibriums of the Same. It must consist and realize itself in the unique throw of the dice. Thus, this throw of the dice is not, in its numerical result, the af- firmation of its own probability or improbability. It is the absolute affirmation of chance as such. It is "the affirmation of all chance in a single moment" (ibid.); it is *the* throw of the dice that has the power of "affirming Chance, of thinking all chance, which is above all not a principle, but the absence of all principle" (*The Fold*, p. 67; translation modified). With each throw of the dice (with each event), there is, no doubt, the formal distinction of numerical results. But the innermost power of the cast is unique and univocal, it is the Event, just as it is what affirms in a unique Throw, which is the Throw of all the throws, the totality of chance. The numerical results are only superficial stampings or simulacra of the Great Cast.

3. One begins to see where the eternal return fits in. What eter- nally returns in each event, in all the divergences and all the disjunctive syntheses, what returns each time the dice are cast, is the *original unique throw of the dice with the power of affirming chance*. In all the throws, the same Throw returns, because the being of the cast is invariable *in its productive determination:* to affirm all chance in a single moment.

As is very often the case with Deleuze, the joint salvation of two concepts threatened by the "Platonism" of the Same (here, chance and the eternal return) is found in the pure and simple identification of these concepts. What is "the eternal return itself" (*The Logic of Sense*, p. 180)? It is, Deleuze immediately tells us, "the affirmation of all chance in a single moment, the unique cast for all throws, one Being and only one for all forms and all times, a single insistence for all that exists" (ibid.; translation modified).

Ultimately, the eternal return is the One as the affirmation of chance, or affirma- tion of the fact that chance is affirmed in a single throw, which returns as the active being of all casts, of all fortuitous events. But one can just as well say that chance is the One as eternal return, for what makes an event fortuitous is that it has as its unique active power, as its generic virtuality, that which returns—namely, the original Great Cast.

The conclusion of this logic is no doubt a virtual doctrine of contingency. That which insists in, and returns eternally to, all the immanent events of the power of the One is chance *as the chance of the One itself.* And what are we to understand by "the chance of the One," if not the radical contingency of Being? All in all, the eternal return is the univocal affirmation, deployed in all the events that auto-affect Being, of the latter's own contingency. And here we equally refind the logic of sense. For the fact that univocity, as we know, is the univocity of the distribution of sense according to nonsense, can equally be put in the following way: in every event of sense, there returns eternally its having been produced by nonsense.

Nietzsche or Mallarmé

In a letter written at the very end of 1993, touching on the concept of the undecidable that both of us use, although in very different ways, Deleuze took up the question of the dice throw in its direct connection with the virtual. He stated that the undecidable concerns the emissions of virtuals as pure events, as exemplified by the throw of the dice. And he declared once again, extremely clearly, that the different casts of virtuals can be formally distinct, even while they remain the forms of a single and same cast. The result is that the different casts are undecidable and that no decision is the final one—for all decisions communicate and are mutually compounded.

In reflecting on Deleuze's persistent use, since the end of the sixties, of such quasi-identical formulations, I said to myself that the indiscernibility of casts (of events, of emissions of the virtual) was, for him, the most important of the points of passage of the One. For me, on the other hand, the absolute onto-logical separation of the event, the fact that it occurs *in* the situation without being in anyway virtualizable, is the basis of the character of truths as irreducibly original, created, and fortuitous. And if a truth is indiscernible, it is not at all so with respect to other truths (from which it is, on the contrary, doubly discernible: by the situation in which it is inscribed, and by the event that initiates it), but with respect to the resources of discernment proper to the situation in which it originates. For were a truth discernible by the means of these resources, then, in this situation, it would be neither a creation nor a chance.

Contrary to Deleuze, therefore, I think that the "event dice throws" are all absolutely distinct—not formally (on the contrary, the form of all events is the same) but ontologically. This ontological multiplicity does not compose any series, it is sporadic (events are rare) and cannot be totalized. No count can group the events, no virtual subjects them to the One. And, given that there is no series, there is no possibility either that the return of the Same could be brought about through probability. Consequently, I do not believe in any of the possible senses of the eternal return of the Same: the Parmenidian (the permanence of the One), the cosmological (the law of the Same imposed on chaos), the probabilistic (an equilibrium arising at the infinity of a series), or the Nietzschean–Deleuzian sense (affirmation of all chance in a single moment).

At the time of the controversy, materialized by our correspondence, this intimate *disputatio* on the eternal return took (for me) the form of a meditation on our respective conceptions of chance. If, when all is said and done, chance is the affirmation, for Deleuze, of the contingency of the One in all its immanent effects, it is, for me, the predicate of the contingency of *each* event. For Deleuze, chance is the play of the All, always replayed as such; whereas I believe that there is the multiplicity (and rarity) of chances, such that the chance of an event happens to us already by chance, and not by the expressive univocity of the One.

During the summer of 1994, I underlined the degree to which our views on chance were opposed. For, while it remains for him the play of localized folds of the All, for me, given that the void of Being only occurs at the surface of a situation by way of the event, chance is the very matter of a truth. And just as truths are singular and incomparable, so the fortuitous events from which they originate must be multiple and separated by the void. Chance is plural, which excludes the unicity of the dice throw. It is by chance that a particular chance happens. All in all, the contingency of Being is only completely realized if there is also the Chance of chances. But, for Deleuze, insofar as contingency falls under the law of the One, it is realized in a single stroke. The Chance of chances does not exist—and this is the price paid for Being to be full.

We find, on the one hand, a ludic and vital conception of chance; on the other, a stellar conception of the Chance of chance: in sum, Nietzsche or Mallarmé.

On this particular point, Deleuze did not pursue the discussion in detail. I take it up here, but find the fact that he is no longer there to rejoin somewhat disconcerting. How I would so like him to point out to me once again, as he did with great relish in so many different passages, to what extent my philosophy has a reflexive, negative, or analogical value — by which he meant an antivalue, a constellation of the most dire faults — and that it forms a transcendence, with all the attributes of the Kantian Idea! For me, alas! — contrary to his own heroic conviction, based on the incorporation within the One and the unicity of chance — death is not, and can never be, an event.

S E V E N

The Outside and the Fold

WHAT IS thinking? We know that this has always been the central question of philosophy. We also know that the answer must be interlaced with another question: what is Being? And third, since Parmenides, we know that, whatever might be the conceptual elaboration of this interlacement or the proposed answer to the question of Being, in the end it necessarily comes down to the possible modalities of a single statement: "The Same is at once thinking and being."[1]

The greatness of Heidegger consists in his having succinctly reformulated these imperatives as those that define the exercise of philosophy. There is no contemporary creative philosophical enterprise—including that, for example, of Gilles Deleuze—that does not maintain, in taking into consideration the conditions of our time, these three questions: What is to be understood by Being? What is thinking? How does the essential identity of thinking and Being realize itself? We can say that, for Deleuze, Being is formulated univocally as: One, virtual, inorganic life, immanence, the nonsensical donation of sense, pure duration, relation, eternal return, and the affirmation of chance. As for thinking, this is, for him, disjunctive synthesis and intuition, the casting of dice, the ascetic constraint of a case, and the force of memory.

It remains for us to examine in greater depth the theory of interlacement. In what sense are thinking and Being identical, and what use of identity does this involve? For, in Deleuze's view, the logical identity A = A is inadmissible—qua a category of "Platonism."

An Anti-Cartesianism

There is a long tradition in which the identity of thought and Being is considered as a *principle*. In book *Gamma* of the *Metaphysics*, Aristotle refers the possibility of thinking being qua being to the triad of the principles of identity, noncontradiction, and the excluded middle. Deleuze's conviction is that we can no longer take this path. This is not a question of goodwill: we simply *cannot* any longer. The thought that "conjoins" under principles the being of being and the being of thought is factually denied to us by the state of the world (that is, by Being itself in the contemporary arrangement of its modalities or simulacra): "Nietzsche and Mallarmé have rewarded us with the revelation of a Thought-world that throws dice. But for them the world lacks principle, has lost its principles" (*The Fold*, p. 67).

Must we conclude from this that there is an irremediable disjunction between Being and thought? Certainly not! How could the most radical thinker of the One since Bergson accept such a disjunction? Foucault is to be praised, Deleuze tells us, for accepting, even in the most minute detail of his analyses, that "knowledge is being" (*Foucault*, p. 111). The problem, then, is that of a *nonprincipled* identity of thought and Being.

One can find support here from another great tradition, stemming from Descartes, that situates the question of Being-thinking in a problematic of the subject. This tradition does not require, at least on the face of it, any recourse to the transcendence of principles. The interlacement is realized by presupposing that thought has a subject, a support, and by interrogating this subject as to its being. The being of thought is identified as the being of the subject, while the question of the identity of Being and thought becomes that of the position in Being of the Being-subject. This orientation undoubtedly attains its culmination in Hegel, when he sets for philosophy in its entirety the program of "thinking the Absolute not only as substance, but also, and at the same time, as subject."[2]

Deleuze cannot take this path either—at least not directly. He is essentially opposed to everything that presents itself as a "philosophy of the subject," for a number of converging reasons.

1. One must begin with the univocity of Being and then position the equivocal, as expression or simulacrum, within this—and not vice versa. To isolate ontologically the subject and *then* inquire as to how its being belongs to Being spells the ruin of univocity, which is necessarily a *primary* thesis. On this point,

Deleuze echoes Heidegger's opposition to the "metaphysics" of the subject. Nothing is more foreign to him than the Cogito. For, in his view, whoever begins in this way will never extract himself or herself from the equivocal, and never attain the power of the One. This is clearly the case, moreover, from Descartes (Being is said in several senses, according to extension and thought, the body and the soul, as well as according to God) to Sartre (Being is said as the massiveness of the "in-itself" and as the nothingness of consciousness).

2. Identifying the being of thought with a subject endows this being with a constitutive interiority, which refers both to itself (reflexivity) and to its objects, which are given as being heterogeneous to interiority (negativity). But the being of beings does not tolerate either reflexivity or negativity. Beings are modalities of the One: they are superficial inflections or simulacra. As such, they do not bear any relation to anything whatsoever, are the negative of nothing, and cannot internalize the exterior.

Admittedly—and this is what is at stake in the present chapter—there does ultimately exist a pertinent opposition between the outside and the inside, or, more exactly, a folding of the outside that creates the interiority of a self. However, this interiority, far from being constitutive, is itself constituted: it is a result. It cannot serve to identify thought, which, moreover, is not produced by the self, but is the construction of the self—the *act* of folding (or unfolding). And this act will prove to be absolutely homogeneous to Being, it will prove to be a *fold* of Being.

3. What philosophers of the subject, and in particular phenomenologists, pose as an independent region of Being, or transcendental figure, is only a certain type of simulacrum for Deleuze, which he names "lived experience" (the other type of simulacrum being named "states of affairs"). This region consists only of objects, simple "immobile sections" of duration, which are endowed with specific extrinsic (or spatial) movements. Phenomenologists do not, of course, restrict themselves to objects of the "lived experience" type; they refer these objects to their correlations (the functions of lived experience) and study them, without any recourse to the virtual, on a simple plane of reference. They do for lived experience what positive sciences do for states of affairs: they construct the corresponding horizontal functional relations. Deleuze accepts that there might be a "science" of lived experience, but certainly not a philosophy. At best, the subject is a function, or a network of functions, a functional space of lived experience. The subject *refers* lived experience, but is incapable of immersing it within the virtual, and thereby of intuiting its expressive relation to the One.

All in all, the use of the operator "subject" places thought within a paradigm of the scientific type (the plane of reference)—an insight that amounts to a profound understanding of Descartes. Lacan also observed, although with the quite opposite intention of maintaining and refounding the category of the subject, that there was an intrinsic relation between the Cogito and Galileanism; in his eyes, this relation justified calling the referential subject "the subject of science."

4. For Deleuze, this compulsory correlation between the subject and the (scientific) plane of reference disqualifies equally those who uphold structural objectivism and those who uphold subjectivism. Thinking under the (exalting) constraint of the work of Foucault, Deleuze credits the latter with a diagnosis of the utmost importance, namely, that (scientific) "structures" and the "subject" (as the supposed support of thought and its values) are opposed only in appearance. And it is, moreover, still the case today, particularly today (so long after *The Archaeology of Knowledge*, in which this diagnosis is to be found), that the question under debate concerns "the place and status that are those of the subject within dimensions that are assumed to be not completely structured" (*Foucault*, p. 14; translation modified). We can duly observe that those in favor of an enforced structuring of the economy by the free market ("freedom" that we know, from the admission of its own militants, to be that of a monetary police) and of a single political structuring (representative parliamentary government) are the *same* who, alongside these monumental necessities, advocate the return to a moral and humanitarian subject. It is certain that, "as long as we continue to contrast history directly with structure, we can believe that the subject conserves a sense as a constitutive, receptive and unifying activity" (ibid.; translation modified). Foucault's great merit (but Deleuze, in using the free indirect style, makes it his own) is to have constructed thinking configurations that have nothing to do with the couple formed by structural objectivity and constitutive subjectivity. The "epochs," the historical formations, and the *epistemes*, which are the great unities constructed by Foucault, "escape from both the reign of the subject and the empire of structure" (ibid.). And it is in the very place that is left vacant by this dismissal of the positivist objective-subjective couple that Deleuze installs the question of the interlacement of thought and Being.

The Concept of the Fold

If this interlacement is neither of the order of a (logical) theory of principles, nor of the order of an analytic of the subject, then we find ourselves squarely facing— bereft of arms, as it were—the question that Deleuze poses and which, in light of his ontology, can be formulated as follows: *given that thought is set in motion by dis-*

junctive syntheses, and that it is solicited by beings who are in nonrelation, how can it be in accordance with Being, which is essentially Relation?

We have, then, to reconsider the question—already familiar to us—that sets forth the precise challenge to thought posed by the simulacra: "How, then, is the non-relation a relation?" (*Foucault*, p. 65).

The concept of the fold encapsulates the intuitive trajectory that elucidates this paradox. This trajectory, with its characteristic looping (the "perpetual reconcatenation"), can be set out in four segments. When these segments have been integrally run through (and it is necessary at the end, under the name "fold," to repeat the trajectory at infinite speed), we gain access to "the most rigorous link between the singular and the plural, the neutral and repetition" (ibid., p. 14), and, thus, between thought, which only knows disjointed cases, and Being, which is the eternal return of the Same. It is as though this path were etched along the crest of a mountain: it allows us "to reject simultaneously the form of a consciousness or a subject, and the groundlessness of an undifferentiated abyss" (ibid.; translation modified).

In the contemporary epoch, we have no choice but to hold resolutely fast in the face of the disjunction. We no longer have at our disposal the reconciliatory or unifying power of principles. The modern ascesis consists precisely in exposing thought to the pure and simple unbinding. Nothing resembles anything else, nothing joins up with anything else, everything diverges. Even Being, although it is univocal, is "inaugurally" thought as the One of a chasm. Whence the temptation, which goes hand in hand with that of regrounding everything in a subject, of letting oneself slide into nonthought, into the "groundlessness [*sans-fond*] of an undifferentiated abyss."

Let us take the example of univocal Being under its most Bergsonian name: time. As long as we remain in a simple face to face with time (displaying the stupidity of someone who has as yet not commenced the intuitive trajectory), all that we are able to see is the hiatus between, on the one hand, the configuration of "immobile sections + abstract time," which refers to closed sets, that is, actual objects, and, on the other, the implication of "real movement → concrete duration," which refers to "the unity of a time which endures," and "whose movements are so many mobile sections crossing the closed systems" (*Cinema 1*, p. 11).[3] If the One of Being is only effective in this hiatus (between the open and the closed), how can we avoid believing that it is as nonthought, as experimentation of groundlessness, that thought is in accordance with Being? This is the entire question of the relation between philosophical and mystical intuition—a question that Wittgenstein addressed in terms that favored the mystical.

This is in no way an option favored by Deleuze, for whom affirmative thought remains absolutely imperative. It is like a second ascesis: not only must we affront the disjunction and tackle even its most disconcerting precipices, but, in so doing, we must find ourselves *constrained* to follow the One — and to follow it even as far as the conviction that the nonrelation can be thought as relation. The fortitude of this double ascesis is, for example, what constitutes, in the domain of art, the entire merit of the great contemporary filmmakers. On the one hand, their films *actualize* the disjunction: "In the Straubs, in Syberberg, in Marguerite Duras, the voices emerge . . . like a 'story/history' [*histoire*] without a place, while the visible element . . . presents an empty place without a story/history" (*Foucault*, pp. 64–65). But, on the other hand, their entire genius lies in causing the One to pass into the "irrational break" of the simulacra — not at all by the dialectical effect of a synthesis, or by reducing this hiatus by means of some invisible, ineffable and transcendent principle, but by operating, in the editing, a "perpetual reconcatenation [yet again! but we know that this is but another name for intuition] which takes place over . . . the interstice" (ibid., p. 65; translation modified). And similarly, Foucault's unequaled philosophical force consists, first of all, in carrying the disjunction of the two great registers that encompass all knowledge — the visibilities and the statements — to its peak, and in giving us truth severed in two (just as Nietzsche, we may note in passing, wanted "to sever the history of the world in two").[4] And it would seem that there can be no direct relation between these two halves of the true, such that we find ourselves in danger of committing a radical infidelity of thought with respect to the univocity of Being. For would this not be said differently according to the visible and according to the articulable? What a Platonic temptation this is! But at this moment — and this is the supreme force of Foucault — there intervenes the second ascesis, which is what governs the trajectory, so sorely misunderstood, between *The Order of Things* and *The Care of the Self*. Obey the imperative of the One. Invent concepts that allow the disjunction to be passed *over* — just as, without reducing the gulf between two mountains, one passes over the living torrent that traces, at the bottom of the valley, the movement of their separation. Foucault, instructed here by the Deleuze that he himself had instructed, was to set down that "these two halves of truth must enter into a relation, problematically, at the very moment when the problem of truth denies any possible correspondence or conformity between them" (ibid., p. 64).

Is this second ascesis without any guarantee? Must one wager on the One, when the only thing that can be tested, in accordance with the first ascesis, is the violence of the separation? Not entirely. Certainly, the closed sets that we confront are, by themselves, without any resemblance or conformity. They do not correspond in any way. But *that they are all modalities of the Whole is marked in them, almost imperceptibly, by a point of opening, a slight instability, a microscopic oscillation*. Deleuze remarks that "the whole is not a closed set, but on the contrary that by virtue of which the set is never absolutely closed, never completely sheltered, that which keeps it open somewhere as if by the finest thread which attaches it to the rest of the universe" (*Cinema 1*, p. 10).

I sometimes think that this empirical guarantee of the second ascesis amounts to a sort of theoretical convenience. If, ultimately, the attachment of all objects to the rest of the universe is *marked* on the object itself, then what is the purpose of the first ascesis—that which exposes thought to the absoluteness of the disjunction? Would it not suffice to be attentive to this "somewhere" where the object remains open? And I would, no doubt, make the same objection to this providential marking as to the theory of the two—the virtual and the actual—parts of the object: it sorely puts univocity to the test, by directly assigning the chance of thought to a discernible *division* of its objects. It would seem that it is not very easy to definitively abandon the presuppositions of the dialectic.

But what I like in the formula of Deleuze is its invocation of a "*dis-sheltering*" of the closed set (of the actual object). It endows the second ascesis with a certain style that suits me. Yes, indeed! Thinking a situation always involves *going* toward that, in it, which is the least covered by the shelter that the general regime of things offers it, just as in order to think the situation of France today one must start from the "dis-sheltering" by the state of those who are without papers. This is what, in my own language, I name (without needing for this either the virtual or the Whole) an *event site*. I determine this ontologically (with all the required mathematical formulations) as that which is "on the edge of the void"—that is to say, that which is *almost* withdrawn from the situation's regulation by an immanent norm, or its state.[5] In a situation (in a set), it is like a point of exile where *it is possible* that something, finally, might happen. And I must say that I was very pleased when, in detailing in depth at the start of 1994 the "political" similarities between his thesis of dis-sheltering and my thesis of the event site, Deleuze compared the expression "on the edge of the void" to the *intersection* between the territory (the space of actualization) and the process of deterritorialization (the overflowing of the territory by the event that is the real-virtual of all actualization), which is to say that it is the point at which what occurs can no longer be assigned to either the territory (the site) or the nonterritory, to either the inside or the outside. And it is true that the void has neither an interior nor an exterior.

The second ascesis is indeed conducted from an "intersection," which is the overflowing of a site or the "eventful"[6] opening point of the closed. This is the "finest thread" relating an object to the rest of the universe, and it is in following this thread, like Ariadne, that thought can elucidate the labyrinth, whose portal is the dire disjunction or the (apparently) incurable fracture of all truth by the nonrelation of objects.

Let us retrace this partial trajectory in a different semantic field. When thought exposes itself to the disjunction, it is, as we have seen, like an automaton. Only automatism's neutrality can realize the *choice* of being seized disjunctively by an inflection of the One (to choose, Deleuze tells us, is to be chosen, and this is what is difficult). For the automaton, who has realized the giving up of all interiority, *there is only the outside.* This is why intuition (thinking in its chance of being at one with Being) starts, to employ an expression that has met with a great deal of success, as the "thought of the outside."[7] It would, moreover, be better to express this as the "thought-outside," so that no trace of an intentional relation between thought and the outside subsists.

The outside cannot be confused with anything so commonplace as a sort of external world. The automaton (thinking in its ascesis) is a simulacrum that is without any relation to other simulacra. It is, *itself*, the pure assumption of the outside. As Deleuze notes, concerning the canonical example of cinema (canonical because of what is evident in it: "the material automatism of images" [*Cinema 2*, pp. 178–79]): "The automaton is cut off from the outside world, but there is a more profound outside which will animate it" (ibid., p. 179). We can therefore say that intuition begins as animation by the outside.

But what is the underlying principle of all animation? What populates the impersonal outside; what is it that composes forms therein? Let us call this "element" of the outside "force." The name is appropriate for, inasmuch as it is translated only by a constrained animation or by a setting into motion of the automaton-thought, the outside is only *manifest* as the imposition of a force. One of Deleuze's most constant themes is, moreover, that we only think when *forced* to think. Let this be a warning to those who would see in Deleuze an apologia for spontaneity: whatever is spontaneous is inferior to thought, which only begins when it is constrained to become animated by the forces of the outside.

Deleuze attributes to Foucault-Deleuze—who is one of his "conceptual personae"—the following discovery: the element that comes from the outside is force. This is because, for Foucault (but, in fact, for Deleuze elucidating Nietzsche and the play of active and reactive forces), "force is linked to force, but to the force of the outside, such that it is the outside that 'explicates' the exteriority of forms, both for each one and for their mutual relation (*Foucault*, p. 113; translation modified). Thought first plunges into the process of an intuitive apprehension—or, in terms of the One, of the disjunction from which it arises—by constructing a relation, or a diagram of forces, "outside."

The diagram of forces—pure inscription of the outside—does not entail any interiority; it does not as yet communicate with the One as such. It nevertheless causes the disjointed objects (or the regimes of objects, such as the visible and the articulable) to enter into a formal *composition*, which rests characterized by exteriority, but as now activated by its "forceful" seizure. We pass from a simple disjunctive logic of exteriority to a *topology of the outside* as the locus of the inscription of forces that, in their reciprocal action and without communicating between themselves in any way, produce singular exteriorities as a local figure of the outside.

Thought makes of itself a topology of forces of the outside, and in this way has to confront a new question: what are the strata, the diversities, the edges, the connections, that compose this topology? Or again, by what procedure can one *cover* the configurations of forces that populate the outside? Deleuze devotes innumerable pages to this stage of his ontological identification, multiplying the cases and refining the investigations—to such a degree that some have believed him to do nothing other than replace phenomenology by a phenomeno-topology. But this infinite detail is not what matters to us; moreover, to be frank, nor do we find it particularly satisfactory, despite the astounding virtuosity of its variations. What does matter is how the intuition goes beyond the setting up of the topology of forces toward the *act* of its identity with the One.

This movement of the intuition involves topological concepts—concepts that *profoundly* think the outside as a space of forces. The intuitive identification of thinking and Being is realized, for Deleuze, as the topological densification of the outside, which, as such, is carried up to the point that the outside proves to envelop an inside. It is at this moment that thought, in first following this enveloping (from the outside to the inside) and then developing it (from the inside to the outside), is an ontological coparticipant in the power of the One. It *is* the fold of Being.

The pivotal topological operator here is, as one might expect, that of the limit. As soon as the disjunction is thought as the production of exteriority by the forces of the outside, it is equally seen to be the *line* dividing the fields of force, the resultant, traced in the space of the outside, of the exterior forms that deploy the forces. We have already seen that editing, in modern films, makes of cinema-time the tracing-crossing over of an irrational line that externalizes what is said in relation to what is seen. Cinema-time is therefore the creation of a limit, or rather: it constructs in the outside a limit where the nonrelation refers its terms to each other, *because their disjunction is topologically active as a production (i.e., the production precisely of the limit)*. Further, given that thought is nothing other than a construction (because the intuition is identical to its trajectory), it is necessary to state that, by constructing limits, thought already coincides with the disjunction as inflection, or with the nonrelation as relation.

Let us take up again, in this context, the case-Foucault. What is impersonal and automatic in the thought-of-Foucault lies in its having fully exposed itself to the disjunction, in its having absolutely separated, in Being-knowledge, the two halves of the true (language and the visible). Foucault — that inspired theorist of exteriority — was to ascetically install, by a formidable archival labor, each knowledge-form in the topologized outside, which is to say that he forced (or, what comes to the same thing, he was forced by) each form — statements and visibilities, speech and sight — to attain its specific limit, with the two forms becoming thereby positioned in a mutual exteriority. It is in this way that the play of the forces of the outside was constructed: "each reaches its own specific limit which separates it from the other, a visible element that can only be seen, an articulable element that can only be spoken" (ibid., p. 65; translation modified). But, in being constructed in this way, the topology of the outside is such that "the specific limit that separates each one is also the common limit that links one to the other, a limit with two irregular faces, a blind word and a mute vision" (ibid.; translation modified).

One could obviously object that this is a precarious solution. If the One is given as a disjunctive limit or as the tracing of a limit *on* the space of the outside, do we not still have to distinguish between the topology of the space, the One of the topology, and what is inscribed there according to lines of force that Deleuze sometimes describes as "floating" — that is, mobile and abandoned to space, but nevertheless, as results that can be inscribed on its surface, distinct from the outside itself?

At this point, Deleuze's constructive intuition appears to me to be in its properly Mallarméan stage. The difference between the disjunction and the One; or, if one prefers, between the difference of the simulacra and the One of the difference itself; or the difference between the immobile sections of duration and the qualitative change of the Whole; or again, the difference between the difference of the dice throws and the unique cast that haunts and founds them; or yet again, the difference between the divergence of the series and the eternal return: in sum, the difference between the nonrelation and the Relation—all this is reduced to *almost nothing*, to what Mallarmé thinks of as the zero difference between the blank whiteness of the page and the tracings that affect it. This is a difference that is not one, because two tracings only differ insofar as a blank constitutes a limit between them, and reciprocally, two blanks without tracings are indiscernible. And, no doubt, Mallarmé leaves it at that. Being is only "the empty page which its whiteness protects,"[8] except that the being-white of the page can only be thought on the basis of the (trace's) event. For my part, I am Mallarméan: being qua being is only the multiple-composition of the void, except that it follows from the event alone that there can be truths of this void or empty ground.

However, for Deleuze, this solution still concedes too much to the negative. If the limit can only be thought as a mobile trace affecting the outside, it is not certain that we can save univocity. For Being would still be said according to two senses: the outside and the limit, space and the trace, being and event. Thus it is necessary for the act of thought to correspond to the surface (the outside), *as to what is, in itself, the limit.*

But what is simultaneously the movement of a surface and the tracing of a limit, if not, precisely, a fold? If you fold a sheet of paper, you determine a traced line where the folding takes place, which, although it certainly constitutes the common limit of the two subregions of the sheet, is not, however, a tracing *on* the sheet, black on white. For what the fold presents as a limit on the sheet as pure outside is, in its being, a movement of the sheet *itself*.

The most profound moment of the intuition is, therefore, when the limit is thought as fold, and when, as a result, exteriority becomes reversed into interiority. The limit is no longer what affects the outside, it is a fold of the outside. It is auto-affection of the outside (or of force: it amounts to the same). We might as well say that we finally reach the point where the disjunction is intuited as a simple modality of the One: the common limit of the heterogeneous forces that absolutely externalize the objects, or forms, is the very action of the One as self-folding. Thinking coincides with Being when it is a fold (the construction of a limit as a fold) whose living essence is the fold of Being. The ascesis that impersonalizes thought, delivers it to the outside, and subjects it to force assumes its entire sense (which is sense *itself*) when it "discover[s] this outside as a limit, the final horizon against which being begins to fold" (ibid., p. 113; translation modified).

That there is a fold of the outside (that the outside folds itself) ontologically signifies that it creates an inside. Let us imagine the folded sheet: there is an immanent limit on the sheet, but there is also the creation of an internal pocket.

We can therefore state that the intuition in which Being coincides with thinking is the creation, as the fold of the outside, of a figure of the inside. And it is then possible to name this folding a "self"—this is Foucault's concept—and even, if one insists, a subject. Except that we must immediately add: first, that this subject *results* from a topological operation that can be situated in the outside, and that it is thus in no way constitutive, or autonomous, or spontaneous; second, that this subject, as the "inside-space," is not separate from the outside (whose fold it is), or yet again, that it is "completely co-present with the outside-space on the line of the fold" (ibid., p. 118; *see the selection of texts* [Appendix: "The Thought of the Outside"]); and, third, that it only exists as thought, and thus as the process of the double ascesis (in which one must endure the disjunction and hold on to the imperceptible thread of the One), which alone renders it capable of *becoming* the limit as fold.

On these conditions, we can say that *the subject (the inside) is the identity of thinking and being.* Or again, that "To think is to fold, to double the outside with a coextensive inside" (ibid.).

In stating this, we do not at all distance ourselves from Bergson's idea of the intuition (and thus of thought) as the intuition of duration. For (and this furnishes further proof of what I have called the *monotony* of Deleuze's work, of his insistence—which is equally fidelity to the One) the Fold is finally "subjective" because it is exactly the same as Memory, that great total memory that we have seen to be one of the names of Being. Inasmuch as pure duration is the integral conservation of the being of the past, or of the past as Being, memory cannot be assigned to the operation of a subject. Rather, one should speak of a "memory of the outside" (ibid., p. 107), which is the being of time and of which the subject is only a modality. It is then possible to simultaneously understand that "the folding... is itself a Memory" and that "time as subject, or rather subjectivation, is called memory" (ibid.). This confirms that, at the point of the fold, thought and time are the same thing, and as a result, because we know that time is only one of its names, that thought is identical to Being. And it is remarkable that one can name this identity "subject" without having conceded anything to the Cartesian filiation. For, to be a subject is "to think the outside as time, on the condition of the fold" (ibid., p. 108; translation modified).

Both the forceful originality and (for me) the relative lack of seduction of the doctrine of the fold are perhaps best indicated by the consequences of a political nature that follow from it.

On the one hand, given that it can be identified as memory, the fold causes a supple inflection or curving of what has been integrally conserved by the One to prevail at the heart of every creation (or action, or even revolution). The fold makes every thought an immanent trait of the already-there, from which it follows that everything new is an enfolded selection of the past. It is obviously in conformity with the doctrine of the eternal return, of which the fold is, so to speak, an "epistemological variant," that the maxim here is to make "the past active and present to the outside so that something new will finally come about" (ibid., p. 119). As we know, it is essential that every commencement be a recommencement and that memory prove to be "the necessity of recommencing" (ibid., p. 108; translation modified). The extreme — or, one might say, maximal — attention that Deleuze gives to the most radically new forms of art and psychiatry, of science and the movement of different politics, cannot lead us to ignore that, under the jurisdiction of the One, the *thought* of the new plunges the latter into that part of it which is its virtual-past. We would even maintain that it was necessary for Deleuze to acquaint himself, in a spirit of patient curiosity, with the creations of his time and to treat these as cases *so as to* test that they were never absolute beginnings, that they too — and indeed, as foldings and unfoldings of Being, that they especially — were only auto-affections of the immutable One (immutable qua perpetual mutation).

On the other hand, if thought is identical with the One, it, too, must be essentially one. It is necessary that thought be univocal. Thus, there are not really thoughts *in the plural*, and, when all is said and done, it is philosophy or philosophy-art — for philosophy is given in fusion with its indiscernible companion, art, no less for Deleuze than for Nietzsche — that alone maintains immanence and conducts the circuit of the double ascesis through right to the end, thus fully meriting the name of thought. Deleuze's gesture here does not vary: "We are discovering new ways of folding, akin to new envelopments, but we all remain Leibnizian because what always matters is folding, unfolding, refolding" (*The Fold*, p. 137).

As for myself, however, I cannot bring myself to think that the new is a fold of the past, or that thinking can be reduced to philosophy or a single configuration of its act. This is why I conceptualize absolute beginnings (which requires a theory of the void) and singularities of thought that are incomparable in their constitutive gestures (which requires a theory — Cantorian, to be precise — of the plurality of the types of infinity). Deleuze always maintained that, in doing this, I fall back into transcendence and into the equivocity of analogy. But, all in all, if the only way to think a political revolution, an amorous encounter, an invention of the sciences, or a creation of art as distinct infinities—having as their condition in-commensurable separative events—is by sacrificing immanence (which I do not ac-tually believe is the case, but that is not what matters here) and the univocity of Being, then I would sacrifice them. If, in order to render eternal one of those rare frag-ments of truth that traverse here and there our bleak world (but in this, our world is like any other), it is necessary to restrict oneself to the Mallarméan doctrine of the trace (which I do not believe either), then I would do so. If, against the ascesis of the fold, it is necessary to uphold that the fidelity to an event is the militant recollec-tion—transiently obscure and reduced to its actuality—of a generic multiplicity without any underlying virtuality, then I would do so. And, in fact, I do. As Deleuze would have said, in immediately taking up again, just as I would myself, the thread of the argument and the desire to seduce or to win the other over: it is a question of taste.

EIGHT

A Singularity

IN ORDER to situate Deleuze, it is no doubt necessary to turn to his own doctrine concerning the figures of communication between a disjointed singularity and the All. One starts off from the narrowest diagram of forces, from the edges, and follows the "small circuit," before plunging into the most composite virtualities, which are, at the same time, those that circulate and interpenetrate each other; there one follows the "large circuit," in activating absolute memory until, by way of a local inflection of philosophy's entire past, Deleuze appears as a fine point or a crystal that is at once translucent and timeless — just like the crystal balls of clairvoyants.

Whereas philosophy's task is to determine in the concept that which is opposed to opinions, it is nevertheless true that opinion returns, such that there exist philosophical opinions. These can be recognized by the fact that they form sorts of referential and labeled blocs, capable of being harnessed by almost any ideological operation whatsoever, and that all the fuss around their respective positions (which is where the small fry come to the fore) only serves, in fact, to shape, under the heading of "debate," a sort of shoddy *consensus*.

It is one of the signs of Deleuze's greatness that, in spite of his success, he was unable to be incorporated into the major blocs of opinion that organize the petty parliamentary life of the profession. Undoubtedly, between 1969 and 1975, he was the mentor of that fraction of leftism for which all that mattered was desiring machines and nomadism, the sexual and the festive, free flux and the freedom of expression, the so-called free radio stations along with all the other spaces of freedom, the rainbow of minuscule differences, and the molecular protestation fascinated by the powerful molar configurations of Capital. We have already said enough for any and all to understand that this transitory jurisdiction was based on a crucial *misunderstanding*. That Deleuze never did anything of an explicit nature to dissipate this is linked to that weakness rife among philosophers—in fact, none of us escape it— regarding the equivocal role of *disciples*. As a general rule, disciples have been won over for the wrong reasons, are faithful to a misinterpretation, overdogmatic in their exposition, and too liberal in debate. They almost always end up by betraying us. And yet, we seek them out, encourage them, and love them. The reason for this is that philosophy, as a pure act of language whose only effect is internal (as Althusser said, the effects of philosophy are strictly philosophical), obtains a certain satisfaction from the fragment of collective reality that the following of disciples offers it. And we should add that Deleuze, more than anyone else, was sensitive to that vocation[1] of philosophy which, since the trial of Socrates, has notoriously consisted in the corruption of youth. This means that youth must be wrested away from the places and the propositions that every polis preforms in order to ensure its succession. But, as we all know from experience, it is a delicate matter to ensure that it is not via the *wrong side* of a work that this "corruption" takes effect and, thus, turns into its opposite: cynicism. There does, in fact, exist a cynical Deleuzianism, poles apart from the sobriety and asceticism of the Master.

However, this is of little importance. What does matter is that, grasped in the extreme *severity* of his conceptual construction, Deleuze remains tangential to all the blocs of philosophical opinion that have composed the intellectual scene since the 1960s. He was neither a phenomenologist nor a structuralist, neither a Heideggerian nor an importer of Anglo-American analytic "philosophy," nor again a liberal (or neo-Kantian) neohumanist. Which comes to the same thing, in our dear old France where everything is decided politically, as saying that he was neither a fellow traveler of the French Communist Party, nor a Leninist reformer, nor a distressed prophet of the "withdrawal" from the political sphere, nor a moralist of the rights of enlightened Western man. As with all great philosophers, and in perfect conformity with the aristocratism of his thought and his Nietzschean principles of the evaluation of active force, Deleuze constitutes a polarity *all by himself*.

Throughout this tormented period (of declining colonial wars, Gaullism, May '68 and the red years, the Mitterrandian Restoration, and the collapse of the socialist states, among other things), Deleuze inflexibly *absorbed* the diversity of experience within an apparatus that allowed him to pass, by the subterranean passages of the virtual, from the leftist public scene to a sort of ironic solitude, without ever having to modify his categories. That the One could be folded according to eventful declensions with nomadic significance was something that delighted, but did not overly concern, him; that the One could be unfolded according to strongly sedentary closed sets came as no surprise. He was a man of neither untimely and precarious enthusiasms nor nihilistic abdications. Of all the philosophies that have counted in France over the last three decades, his has certainly been the least fundamentally affected by the sharply contrasting stages of our public life. He was to proffer neither any form of proclamation nor repentance. For he had only one authentic intellectual passion, which was to pursue his work according to the rigorous intuitive method that he had laid down once and for all. The infinite multiplicity of cases composing the vivacity of the epoch was no doubt necessary for this; but, above all, it required the incomparable tenacity to treat them uniformly, in accordance with the terrible law of the univocity of Being.

This is to be attributed to his refined Bergsonism, for which, in the final instance, it is always what is that is right. Life makes the multiplicity of evaluations possible, but is itself impossible to evaluate. It can be said that there is nothing new under the sun because everything that happens is only an inflection of the One, the eternal return of the Same. It can equally be said that everything is constantly new because it is only through the perpetual creation of its own folds that the One, in its absolute contingency, can indefinitely return. These two judgments are ultimately indiscernible. We must then wager, in the same sense as does the country priest at the end of Bernanos's book, but without needing for this any other God than the God of Spinoza (Nature): "What does it matter? All is grace."[2] Which has to be punctuated as follows: "All" *is* grace. For what is, is nothing other than the grace of the All.

This wager governed Deleuze's admirable creative Stoicism throughout the inhuman experience of the loss of breath, of immobilized life ("all is grace," even to die). But it was already apparent in his oblique, although concentrated, way of participating in institutional or collective peripeteias with what I would like to name an indifferent cheerfulness ("What does it matter?"). This shows the power of Deleuze's philosophical choice.

Except that, for those like myself who rule out that Being can be thought as All, to say that all is grace means precisely that we are never ever accorded any grace. But this is not correct. It does *occur*, by interruption or by supplement, and however rare or transitory it may be, we are forced to be *lastingly* faithful to it.

But let us leave the dispute there. During this (short) period of our philosophical history, all in all there have only been (there are still only) two serious questions: that of the All (or the One) and that of grace (or the event). It is precisely because he obstinately confronted these questions, under the paired forms of the eternal return and chance, that Deleuze is a great contemporary thinker.

Let us now consider the second circle, that of philosophy in France over the last century. An ordered and rational vision of its development is most often rendered impossible because of the smoke screen raised by the confrontations between blocs of opinion. Between Marxism and existentialism, structuralism and humanism, spiritualism and materialism, "new" philosophy and Leninist revolutionaries, Christian personalists and lay progressives, adepts and adversaries of the "linguistic turn," or analytic and hermeneutical perspectives, how is it possible to set up a significative system of reference that draws on concepts rather than figures, philosophy rather than philosophemes?

Let us suppose that the history of this period is guided by the coupling of two proper names: Bergson and Brunschvicg.[3] We find, on the one hand, the concrete intuition of time, carried as far as a metaphysics of living totality, and, on the other, the timeless intuition of mathematical idealities, carried as far as a metaphysics of creative Reason. On the one hand, a metaphorizing phenomenology of pure change; on the other, a historicized axiomatics of the construction of eternal truths. Or again, on the one hand, a depreciation of the abstract as a simple instrumental convenience, and, on the other, an apologia of the Idea as the construction in which thought is revealed to itself. And finally, on the one hand, an exaltation of the dynamic coincidence with the Open, and, on the other, an organized distrust in respect to everything that cannot be specified as a closed set, signed by a concept.

So solid were these two great speculative frameworks that the progressive penetration of the great German texts (Hegel, Husserl, Heidegger) into the French university took place more by incorporation within this pair of dominant traditions than by a veritable disjunctive "outcome." Two striking examples can be cited in this respect: Albert Lautman gave an altogether singular interpretation of Heidegger that assimilated the latter to the mathematizing Platonism that Lautman had inherited from Brunschvicg;[4] and Sartre read Husserl in such a way that, on the basis of the intentional theory of consciousness, he shaped a concept of freedom that was metaphysically isomorphic to Bergsonian "life"—to the point that the opposition between the closed and the open was still to govern, from beginning to end, the *Critique of Dialectical Reason*.

Deleuze's immense merit was to have assumed and modernized the Bergsonian filiation. With a sovereign indifference to the successive fashions that disguised their adherence to the tradition under the gaudy veneer of ostentatious importation, he confronted the operators of Bergson with the concrete artistic, scientific, or political productions of our time. He tested the intuitive reliability of these operators, completing and transforming them whenever their subjection to the test of cases proved this to be necessary. Above all, he extricated Bergson from what the latter had laid himself much too open to, in the way of a recuperation of the injunctions of the Open by Christian spiritualism and an adjustment of his cosmic vision to a certain global teleology of which Father Teilhard de Chardin was for a time the herald. One can therefore say that Deleuze single-handedly succeeded in carrying out, without any kind of concession, an astonishing undertaking that consisted in integrally secularizing Bergsonism and in connecting its concepts to the creations at the forefront of our time. In so doing, he constructed the most solid barrier possible against the threat facing us of the hegemonic penetration of Anglo-American scholasticism, which has, as its twin props, the logic of ordinary language, on the epistemological side, and the parliamentary moral doctrine of rights, on the pragmatic side. Against all this, Deleuze's stubborn subtlety opposes a *non possumus* without appeal.

The problem, no doubt, is that this barrier remains external, in that it does not support the real rights of the abstract. In presupposing that the intuition is internal to the immanent changes of the One, it cannot avoid continually depreciating what there is of conceptual stability in the order of theory, of formal equilibrium in the order of art, amorous consistency in the existential order, and organization in the political. However seductive the scintillations of concrete analysis may be, however tempting it is to lay down one's arms before the sweeping tide of actualization with its progressive dissolution of all objects, as though these were nothing but the simple traces of its passage on the sand, the fact nevertheless remains that the entire edifice is vulnerable to the powers of decomposition that our grandiose and decaying capitalism liberates on a large scale.

There remains to be built, by way of a second line, as it were, an internal barrier that, drawing on the resources of logic, mathematics, and abstraction (against logicizing "grammaticalism"), as well as on those of organized emancipatory politics (against "democratic" consensus), enables thought to resist. But this time, one must have recourse to the other tradition that, beyond the French masters, goes back, not to Nietzsche and the Stoics, but to Descartes and Plato.

This opens us to the third circle, which is that of the entire history of philosophy. In his elucidation of the final Foucault—the Foucault who returned to the Greeks—Deleuze was to explain that thought must ultimately submit itself to this long span in which consists, in fact, our veritable time.

It is a sign of Deleuze's genius that he constructed an entirely original genealogy of his philosophy. Whether one considers the admirable monographs on Spinoza, Leibniz, Hume, Kant, Bergson, and Nietzsche, or the expositions, in free indirect style, that reconstitute the Stoics, Lucretius, or Whitehead *within* an intuitive trajectory or the construction of a concept (it is the same thing), one finds that they form a history whose singularity is that of Deleuze's own virtuality and which embeds the actuality of his writing within a circuit where the whole of philosophy is treated as an absolute detemporalized memory. The result is that Deleuze's "historian" style cuts across the classical opposition between objectivist history and interpretative history. It is a style in which the most precise knowledge of texts and contexts is inseparable from the movement by which they are drawn toward Deleuze. It partakes neither of archives nor of hermeneutics. For at issue is one thing alone, namely, that great conceptual creations *return*. And the singularity of Deleuze functions as a power of reception for this return. This is why his philosophy can restore Spinoza, Bergson, or Nietzsche to their exact eternity, which is never anything other than that of their *power*—and as such, an eternity that is living only when actualized in living thought.

That it is thinkers of the One, or of immanence, or of univocity, who are gathered together in the Deleuzian virtuality should hardly surprise us. That the designated enemies are the architects of transcendence ("Platonism"), or, even worse, those who inject the transcendence of the Concept into a fake immanence (Hegel), goes without saying. In reference to his monograph on Kant, Deleuze himself explained that it was an exercise in counterproof: the testing of his thought's intuitive power of evaluation on an "enemy" (on a veritably heterogeneous inflection of the One). I was able to gauge personally that this was really the case, for, in our private polemic, the epithet "neo-Kantian" was the crushing accusation that Deleuze most often tried to pin on me.

The fact remains that Deleuze is no doubt the first philosopher to have *activated* in this way, as a division of memory, the ahistorical history of the One-thought. We are dealing here with a veritable creation, whose only equivalent in this century is the historical[5] assemblage of Heidegger.

The main reason these two constructions are so different is that Deleuze does not decipher any destiny, or, rather, that for him destiny is never anything other than the integral affirmation of chance. Accordingly, he readily declared that he had no problem of the "end of philosophy" kind, which I take to mean (agreeing with him without reserve on this point) that the construction of a metaphysics remains the philosopher's ideal, with the question being not "Is it still possible?" but "Are we capable of it?"

It is all the more symptomatic therefore that the crucial point at which Deleuze intersects with Heidegger is in their ineluctable devaluation of Plato — which both get from Nietzsche.

As far as philosophical genealogy is concerned, there is no doubting the validity of the proverb "Tell me what you think of Plato, and I will tell you who you are." From a technical point of view, one can establish that the protocol of evaluation of Platonism is not, for Deleuze, *essentially* different from that which one finds in Heidegger's work. For this involves, as much for the one as for the other, locating *the construction of a transcendence as an unfolding*. Deleuze recognizes Heidegger as having been a great thinker of the fold of Being, identified as the fold of being and beings. In Heidegger's view, Plato orchestrated the separating *unfolding* that distributes beings and being into two distinct regions (for example, the sensible and the intelligible). The fold is no longer anything more than a trait, isolating the Idea from its realizations. The result is that everything is put into place for Being to be thought as a supreme being, be this God or Man. It suffices to *orient* the plane and to organize the regions into a hierarchy — which it is impossible to do if the regions remain folded. Deleuze does not say anything different from this, except insofar as he insists on the *power* of folding, and views the Platonic unfolding as a weakness, a procedure of reactive force. The result is that although the Platonic gesture founds, for Heidegger, an absolute historical *archē* (the destiny of metaphysics), for Deleuze, everything is constantly replayed, the dice are recast, the Throw of the dice returns. The Stoics, Spinoza, Nietzsche, Bergson, as well as Deleuze himself, will construct the fold of the unfolding, will refold, will virtualize. Platonism is not a destiny; it is a necessary counterdestiny, the outcome of the dice confused with the unique cast, the power of the open forced back onto closed distributions. Platonism will never cease to be overturned, because it has, from the very beginning, been overturned. Deleuze is the contemporary point of passage for the return of this overturning.

But perhaps the imperative is completely different: that it is not Platonism that has to be overturned, but the anti-Platonism taken as evident throughout the entire century. Plato has to be *restored*, and first of all by the deconstruction of "Platonism" — that common figure, montage of opinion, or configuration that circulates from Heidegger to Deleuze, from Nietzsche to Bergson, but also from Marxists to positivists, and which is still used by the counterrevolutionary New Philosophers (Plato as the first of the totalitarian "master thinkers"), as well as by neo-Kantian moralists. "Platonism" is the great fallacious construction of modernity and postmodernity alike. It serves as a type of general negative prop: it only exists to legitimate the "new" under the heading of an anti-Platonism.

Certainly, the anti-Platonism proposed by Deleuze is the most generous and the most progressive, the least inclined to evoke a destining agency and the most open to contemporary creations. All that Deleuze lacked was to finish with anti-Platonism itself.

The reason, no doubt, is that he was, just like Heidegger, a preSocratic. Not, however, in the sense of a Parmenidian, or a poet of the inaugural unconcealment of Being; rather, Deleuze was a pre-Socratic in the sense that the Greeks themselves referred to these thinkers: as *physicists*, by which we are to understand "thinkers of the All." Yes, Deleuze will prove to have been our great physicist: he who contemplated the fire of the stars for us, who sounded the chaos, took the measure of inorganic life, and immersed our meager circuits in the immensity of the virtual. It may be said of him that he did not support the idea that "the great Pan is dead."

Now, in his own way, Plato conducted the trial against philosophy construed as a Great Physics. He gave thought the means to refer to itself as philosophical, independently of any total contemplation of the Universe or any intuition of the virtual.

There is in Deleuze, as in every physicist of this kind, a great power of speculative dreaming and something akin to a quivering tonality that is prophetic, although without promise. He said of Spinoza that he was the Christ of philosophy. To do Deleuze full justice, let us say that, of this Christ and his inflexible announcement of salvation by the All—a salvation that promises nothing, a salvation that is always *already there*—he was truly a most eminent apostle.

Selected Texts by Gilles Deleuze

The following extracts from some of Gilles Deleuze's books are not at all presented under the guise of a selection of the "most beautiful pages" ever written by Deleuze, who was, as is well known, a remarkable writer. Their sole function is to situate the references on which the preceding essay primarily draws within a slightly wider context.

The Univocity of Being (I)

From *Difference and Repetition*, translated by Paul Patton (New York: Columbia University Press, 1994), pp. 35–37.

THERE HAS only ever been one ontological proposition: Being is univocal. There has only ever been one ontology, that of Duns Scotus, which gave being a single voice. We say Duns Scotus because he was the one who elevated univocal being to the highest point of subtlety, albeit at the price of abstraction. However, from Parmenides to Heidegger it is the same voice which is taken up, in an echo which itself forms the whole deployment of the univocal. A single voice raises the clamour of being. We have no difficulty in understanding that Being, even if it is absolutely common, is nevertheless not a genus. It is enough to replace the model of judgement with that of the proposition. In the proposition understood as a complex entity we distinguish: the sense, or what is expressed in the proposition; the designated (what expresses itself in the proposition); the expressors or designators, which are numerical modes — that is to say, differential factors characterising the elements endowed with sense and designation. We can conceive that names or propositions do not have the same sense even while they designate exactly the same thing (as in the case of the celebrated examples: morning star-evening star, Israel-Jacob, *planblanc*). The distinction between these senses is indeed a real distinction (*distinctio realis*), but there is nothing numerical — much less ontological — about it: it is a formal, qualitative or semiological distinction. The question whether categories are directly assimilable to such senses, or — more probably — derive from them, must be left aside for the moment. What is important is that we can conceive of several formally distinct senses which none the less refer to being as if to a single designated entity, ontologically one. It is true that such a point of view is not sufficient to prevent us from considering these senses as analogues and this unity of being as an analogy. We must add that being, this common designated, in so far as it expresses itself, is said in turn *in a single and same sense* of all the numerically distinct designators and expressors. In the ontological proposition, not only is that which is designated ontologically the same for qualitatively distinct senses, but also the sense is ontologically the same for individuating modes, for numerically distinct designators or expressors: the ontological proposition involves a circulation of this kind (expression as a whole).

In effect, the essential in univocity is not that Being is said in a single and same sense, but that it is said, in a single and same sense, *of* all its individuating differences or intrinsic modalities. Being is the same for all these modalities, but these modalities are not the same. It is 'equal' for all, but they themselves are not equal. It is said of all in a single sense, but they themselves do not have the same sense. The essence of univocal being is to include individuating differences, while these differences do not have the same essence and do not change the essence of being—just as white includes various intensities, while remaining essentially the same white. There are not two 'paths', as Parmenides' poem suggests, but a single 'voice' of Being, which includes all its modes, including the most diverse, the most varied, the most differenciated. Being is said in a single and same sense of everything of which it is said, but that of which it is said differs: it is said of difference itself.

No doubt there is still hierarchy and distribution in univocal being, in relation to the individuating factors and their sense, but distribution and even hierarchy have two completely different, irreconcilable acceptations. Similarly for the expressions *logos* and *nomos*, in so far as these refer to problems of distribution. We must first of all distinguish a type of distribution which implies a dividing up of that which is distributed: it is a matter of dividing up the distributed as such. It is here that in judgement the rules of analogy are all-powerful. In so far as common sense and good sense are qualities of judgement, these are presented as principles of division which declare themselves *the best distributed*. A distribution of this type proceeds by fixed and proportional determinations which may be assimilated to 'properties' or limited territories within representation. The agrarian question may well have been very important for this organisation of judgement as the faculty which distinguishes parts ('on the one hand and on the other hand'). Even among the gods, each has his domain, his category, his attributes, and all distribute limits and lots to mortals in accordance with destiny. Then there is a completely other distribution which must be called nomadic, a nomad *nomos*, without property, enclosure or measure. Here, there is no longer a division of that which is distributed but rather a division among those who distribute *themselves* in an open space—a space which is unlimited, or at least without precise limits.[1] Nothing pertains or belongs to any person, but all persons are arrayed here and there in such a manner as to cover the largest possible space. Even when it concerns the serious business of life, it is more like a space of play, or a rule of play, by contrast with sedentary space and *nomos*. To fill a space, to be distributed within it, is very different from distributing the space. It is an errant and even 'delirious' distribution, in which things are deployed across the entire extensity of a univocal and undistributed Being. It is not a matter of being which is distributed according to the requirements of representation, but of all things being divided up within being in the univocity of simple presence (the One-All). Such a distribution is demonic rather than divine, since it is a peculiarity of demons to operate in the intervals between the gods' fields of action, as it is to leap over the barriers or the enclosures, thereby confounding the boundaries between properties. Oedipus' chorus cries: 'Which demon has leapt further than the longest leap?' The leap here bears witness to the unsettling difficulties that nomadic distributions introduce into the sedentary structures of representation. The same goes for hierarchy. There is a hierarchy which measures beings according to their limits, and according to their degree of proximity or distance from a principle. But there is also a hierarchy which considers things and beings from the point of view of power: it is not a question of considering absolute degrees of power, but only of knowing whether a being eventually 'leaps over' or transcends its limits in going to the limit of what it can do, whatever its degree. 'To the limit', it will be argued, still presupposes a limit. Here, limit [*peras*] no longer refers to what maintains the thing under a law, nor to what delimits or separates it from other things. On the contrary, it refers to that on the basis of which it is deployed and deploys all its power; hubris ceases to be simply condemnable and *the smallest becomes equivalent to the largest* once it is not separated from what it can do. This enveloping measure is the same for all things, the same also for substance, quality, quantity, etc., since it forms a single maximum at which the developed diversity of all degrees touches the equality which envelops them. This ontological measure is closer to the immeasurable state of things than to the first kind of measure; this ontological hierarchy is closer to the hubris and anarchy of beings than to the first hierarchy. It is the monster which combines all the demons. The words 'everything is equal' may therefore resound joyfully, on condition that they are said *of* that which is not equal in this equal, univocal Being: equal being is immediately present in everything, without mediation or intermediary, even though things reside unequally in this equal being. There, however, where they are borne by hubris, all things are in absolute proximity, and whether they are large or small, inferior or superior, none of them participates more or less in being, nor receives it by analogy. Univocity of being thus also signifies equality of being. Univocal Being is at one and the same time nomadic distribution and crowned anarchy.

The Virtual

From *Difference and Repetition*, translated by Paul Patton (New York: Columbia University Press, 1994), pp. 208–12. Translation modified.

WE HAVE ceaselessly invoked the virtual. In so doing, have we not fallen into the vagueness of a notion closer to the undetermined than to the determinations of difference? It is precisely this, however, that we wished to avoid in speaking of the virtual. We opposed the virtual and the real: although it could not have been more precise before now, this terminology must be corrected. The virtual is opposed not to the real but to the actual. *The virtual is fully real in so far as it is virtual.* Exactly what Proust said of states of resonance must be said of the virtual: 'Real without being actual, ideal without being abstract'; and symbolic without being fictional. Indeed, the virtual must be defined as strictly a part of the real object — as though the object had one part of itself in the virtual into which it plunged as though into an objective dimension. Accounts of the differential calculus often liken the differential to a 'portion of the difference'. Or, following Lagrange's method, the question is asked which part of the mathematical object presents the relations in question and must be considered derived. The reality of the virtual consists of the differential elements and relations along with the singular points which correspond to them. The reality of the virtual is structure. We must avoid giving the elements and relations which form a structure an actuality which they do not have, and withdrawing from them a reality which they have. We have seen that a double process of reciprocal determination and complete determination defined that reality: far from being undetermined, the virtual is completely determined. When it is claimed that works of art are immersed in a virtuality, what is being invoked is not some confused determination but the completely determined structure formed by its genetic differential elements, its 'virtual' or 'embryonic' elements. The elements, varieties of relations and singular points co-exist in the work or the object, in the virtual part of the work or object, without it being possible to designate a point of view privileged over others, a centre which would unify the other centres. How, then, can we speak simultaneously of both complete determination and only a part of the object? The determination must be a complete determination of the object, yet form only a part of it. Following suggestions made by Descartes in his *Replies to Arnaud,* we must carefully distinguish the object in so far as it is complete and the object in so far as it is whole. What is complete is only the ideal part of the object, which participates with other parts of objects in the Idea (other relations, other singular points), but never constitutes an integral whole as such. What the complete determination lacks is the whole set of relations belonging to actual existence. An object may be *ens,* or rather *(non)-ens omni modo determinatum,* without being entirely determined or actually existing.

There is thus another part of the object which is determined by actualisation. Mathematicians ask: What is this other part represented by the so-called primitive function? In this sense, integration is by no means the inverse of differen*t*iation but, rather, forms an original process of differen*c*iation. Whereas differentiation determines the virtual content of the Idea as problem, differenciation expresses the actualisation of this virtual and the constitution of solutions (by local integrations). Differenciation is like the second part of difference, and in order to designate the integrity or the integrality of the object we require the complex notion of differen*t/c*iation. The *t* and the *c* here are the distinctive feature or the phonological relation of difference in person. Every object is double without it being the case that the two halves resemble one another, one being a virtual image and the other an actual image. They are unequal odd halves. Differentiation itself already has two aspects of its own, corresponding to the varieties of relations and to the singular points dependent upon the values of each variety. However, differenciation in turn has two aspects, one concerning the qualities or diverse species which actualise the varieties, the other concerning number or the distinct parts actualising the singular points. For example, genes as a system of differential relations are incarnated at once both in a species and in the organic parts of which it is composed. There is in general no quality which does not refer to a space defined by the singularities corresponding to the differential relations incarnated in that quality. The work of Lavelle and of Nogué, for example, has shown the existence of spaces belonging to qualities and the manner in which these spaces are constructed alongside singularities, so that a difference in quality is always subtended by a spatial difference (*diaphora*). Furthermore, the reflections of painters teach us everything about the space of each colour and the alignment of such spaces within a work. Species are differenciated only in so far as each has parts which are themselves differenciated. Differenciation is always simultaneously differenciation of species and parts, of qualities and extensities: determination of qualities or determination of species, but also partition or organisation. How, then, do these two aspects of differenciation connect with the two preceding aspects of differentiation? How do the two dissimilar halves of an object fit together? Qualities and species incarnate and render actual the varieties of relation; organic parts incarnate the corresponding singularities. However, the precision with which they fit together is better seen from two complementary points of view.

On the one hand, complete determination carries out the differentiation of singularities, but it bears only upon their existence and their distribution. The nature of these singular points is specified only by the form of the neighbouring integral curves—in other words, by virtue of the actual or differenciated species and spaces. On the other hand, the essential aspects of sufficient reason—determinability, reciprocal determination, complete determination—find their systematic unity in progressive determination. In effect, the reciprocity of determination does not signify a regression, nor a marking time, but a veritable progression in which the reciprocal terms must be secured step by step, and the relations themselves established between them. The completeness of the determination also implies the progressivity of adjunct fields. In going from A to B and then B to A, we do not arrive back at the point of departure as in a bare repetition; rather, the repetition between A and B and B and A is the progressive trajectory or description of the whole of a problematic field. It is like Vitrac's poem, where the different steps which each form a poem (Writing, Dreaming, Forgetting, Looking for the opposite, Humourising and finally *Rediscovering by analysing*) progressively determine the whole poem as a problem or a multiplicity. In this sense, by virtue of this progressivity, every structure has a purely logical, ideal or dialectical time. However, this virtual time itself determines a time of differenciation, or rather rhythms or different times of actualisation which correspond to the relations and singularities of the structure and, for their part, measure the passage from virtual to actual. In this regard, four terms are synonymous: actualise, differenciate, integrate and solve. For the nature of the virtual is such that, for it, to be actualised is to be differenciated. Each differenciation is a local integration or a local solution which then connects with others in the overall solution or the global integration. This is how, in the case of the organic, the process of actualisation appears simultaneously as the local differenciation of parts, the global formation of an internal milieu, and the solution of a problem posed within the field of constitution of an organism.[1] An organism is nothing if not the solution to a problem, as are each of its differenciated organs, such as the eye which solves a light 'problem'; but nothing within the organism, no organ, would be differenciated without the internal milieu endowed with a general effectivity or integrating power of regulation. (Here again, in the case of living matter, the negative forms of opposition and contradiction, obstacle and need, are secondary and derivative in relation to the imperatives of an organism to be constructed or a problem to be solved.)

The only danger in all this is that the virtual could be confused with the possible. The possible is opposed to the real; the process undergone by the possible is therefore a 'realisation'. By contrast, the virtual is not opposed to the real; it possesses a full reality by itself. The process it undergoes is that of actualisation. It would be wrong to see only a verbal dispute here: it is a question of existence itself. Every time we pose the question in terms of possible and real, we are forced to conceive of existence as a brute eruption, a pure act or leap which always occurs behind our backs and is subject to the law of all or nothing. What difference can there be between the existent and the non-existent if the non-existent is already possible, already included in the concept and having all the characteristics that the concept confers upon it as a possibility? Existence is *the same* as but outside the concept. Existence is therefore supposed to occur in space and time, but these are understood as indifferent milieux instead of the production of existence occurring in a characteristic space and time. Difference can no longer be anything but the negative determined by the concept: either the limitation imposed by possibles upon each other in order to be realised, or the opposition of the possible to the reality of the real. The virtual, by contrast, is the characteristic state of Ideas: it is on the basis of its reality that existence is produced, in accordance with a time and a space immanent in the Idea.

The possible and the virtual are further distinguished by the fact that one refers to the form of identity in the concept, whereas the other designates a pure multiplicity in the Idea which radically excludes the identical as a prior condition. Finally, to the extent that the possible is open to 'realisation', it is understood as an image of the real, while the real is supposed to resemble the possible. That is why it is difficult to understand what existence adds to the concept when all it does is double like with like. Such is the defect of the possible: a defect which serves to condemn it as produced after the fact, as retroactively fabricated in the image of what resembles it. The actualisation of the virtual, on the contrary, always takes place by difference, divergence or differenciation. Actualisation breaks with resemblance as a process no less than it does with identity as a principle. Actual terms never resemble the virtuality they actualise: the qualities and species no more resemble the differential relations they incarnate than the parts resemble the singularities that they incarnate.[2] In this sense, actualisation or differenciation is always a genuine creation. It does not result from any limitation of a pre-existing possibility. It is contradictory to speak of 'potential', as certain biologists do, and to define differenciation by the simple limitation of a global power, as though this potential were indistinguishable from a logical possibility. For a potential or virtual object, to be actualised is to create divergent lines which correspond to — without resembling — a virtual multiplicity. The virtual possesses the reality of a task to be performed or a problem to be solved: it is the problem which orientates, conditions and engenders solutions, but these do not resemble the conditions of the problem. Bergson was right, therefore, to say that from the point of view of differenciation, even the resemblances which appear along divergent lines of evolution (for example, the eye as an 'analogous' organ) must be related first of all to the heterogeneity in the production mechanism. Moreover, the subordination of difference to identity and that of difference to similitude must be overturned in the same movement. What is this correspondence, however, without resemblance, or creative differenciation? The Bergsonian schema which unites *Creative Evolution* and *Matter and Memory* begins with the account of a gigantic memory, a multiplicity formed by the virtual coexistence of all the sections of the 'cone', each section being the repetition of all the others and being distinguished from them only by the order of the relations and the distribution of singular points. Then, the actualisation of this mnemonic virtual takes the form of the creation of divergent lines, each of which corresponds to a virtual section and represents a manner of solving a problem, but also the incarnation of the order of relations and distribution of singularities peculiar to the given section in differenciated species and parts.[3] Difference and repetition in the virtual ground the movement of actualisation, of differenciation as creation. They are therefore substituted for the identity and the resemblance of the possible, which inspires only a pseudo-movement, the false movement of realisation understood as abstract limitation.

Sense and the Task of Philosophy

From *The Logic of Sense*, translated by Mark Lester with Charles Stivale (New York: Columbia University Press, 1990), pp. 71–73. Translation modified.

AUTHORS REFERRED to as "structuralists" by recent practice may have no essential point in common other than this: sense, regarded not at all as appearance but as surface effect and position effect, and produced by the circulation of the empty square in the structural series (the place of the dummy, the place of the king, the blind spot, the floating signifier, the value degree zero, the off-stage or absent cause, etc.). Structuralism, whether consciously or not, celebrates new findings of a Stoic and Carrollian inspiration. Structure is in fact a machine for the production of incorporeal sense (*skindapsos*). But when structuralism shows in this manner that sense is produced by nonsense and its perpetual displacement, and that it is born of the respective position of elements which are not by themselves "signifying", we should not at all compare it with what was called the philosophy of the absurd: Carroll, yes; Camus, no. This is so because, for the philosophy of the absurd, nonsense is what is opposed to sense in a simple relation with it, so that the absurd is always defined by deficiency of sense and a lack (there is not enough of it...). From the point of view of structure, on the contrary, there is always too much sense: an excess produced and over-produced by nonsense as a lack of itself. Jakobson defines a phoneme zero, having no phonetically determined value, by its opposition to the *absence of the phoneme* rather than to the phoneme itself. Likewise, nonsense does not have any particular sense, but is opposed to the absence of sense rather than to the sense that it produces in excess — without ever maintaining with its product the simple relation of exclusion to which some people would like to reduce them.[1] Nonsense is that which has no sense but, as such, in enacting the donation of sense, is also the very opposite of the absence of sense. This is what we must understand by "*nonsense*".

In the final analysis, the importance of structuralism in philosophy, and for all thought, is that it displaces frontiers. When the emphasis shifted from failing Essences to the notion of sense, the philosophical dividing line seemed to be established between those who linked sense to a new transcendence, a new avatar of God and a transformed heaven, and those who found sense in man and his abyss, a newly excavated depth and underground. New theologians of a misty sky (the sky of Koenigsberg), and new humanists of the caverns, sprang upon the stage in the name of the God-man or the Man-god as the secret of sense. Sometimes it was difficult to distinguish between them. But what today renders the distinction impossible is, first and foremost, our current fatigue with this interminable discourse, in which one wonders whether it is the ass which loads man or man who loads the ass and himself. Moreover, we have the impression of a pure counter-sense imposed on sense; for, in any case, heavenly or subterranean, sense is presented as Principle, Reservoir, Reserve, Origin. As heavenly Principle, it is said to be fundamentally forgotten and veiled or, as subterranean principle, it is said to be deeply erased, diverted, and alienated. But beneath the erasure and the veil, we are summoned to rediscover and to restore meaning, in either a God which was not well enough understood, or in a man not fully fathomed. It is thus pleasing that there resounds today the news that sense is never a principle or an origin, but that it is produced. It is not something to discover, to restore, and to re-employ; it is something to produce by a new machinery. It belongs to no height or depth, but rather to a surface effect, being inseparable from the surface which is its proper dimension. It is not that sense lacks depth or height, but rather that height and depth lack surface, that they lack sense, or have it only by virtue of an "effect" which presupposes sense. We no longer ask ourselves whether the "originary meaning" of religion is to be found in a God betrayed by men, or in a man alienated in the image of God. We do not, for example, seek in Nietzsche a prophet of overturning or transcendence. If there is an author for whom the death of God or the free fall of the ascetic ideal has no importance so long as it is compensated by the false depth of the human, by bad faith and *ressentiment*, it is indeed Nietzsche. He pursues his discoveries elsewhere, in the aphorism and the poem (where neither God nor man speak) in their capacity as machines for the production of sense and for the survey of the surface. Nietzsche establishes the effective ideal game.

We do not seek in Freud an explorer of human depth and originary sense, but rather the prodigious discoverer of the machinery of the unconscious by means of which sense is produced always as a function of nonsense.[2] And how could we not feel that our freedom and strength reside, not in the divine universal nor in the human personality, but in these singularities which are more us than we ourselves are, more divine than the gods, as they animate concretely poem and aphorism, permanent revolution and partial action? What is bureaucratic in these fantastic machines which are peoples and poems? It suffices that we dissipate ourselves a little, that we are able to be at the surface, that we stretch our skin like a drum, in order that the "great politics" begin. An empty square for neither man nor God; singularities which are neither general nor individual, neither personal nor universal. All of this is traversed by circulations, echoes, and events which produce more sense, more freedom, and more strength than man has ever dreamed of, or God ever conceived. Today's task is to make the empty square circulate and to make pre-individual and nonpersonal singularities speak—in short, to produce sense.

The Univocity of Being (II)

From *The Logic of Sense*, translated by Mark Lester with Charles Stivale (New York: Columbia University Press, 1990), pp. 179–80. Translation modified.

PHILOSOPHY MERGES with ontology, but ontology merges with the univocity of being (analogy has always been a theological vision, not a philosophical one, adapted to the forms of God, the world, and the self). The univocity of being does not mean that there is one and the same being; on the contrary, beings are multiple and different, they are always produced by a disjunctive synthesis, and they themselves are disjointed and divergent, *membra disjuncta*. The univocity of being signifies that being is Voice, that it says itself, and that it is said in one and the same "sense" of everything of which it is said. That of which it is said is not all the same, but being is the same for everything of which it is said. It occurs, therefore, as a unique event for everything that happens to the most diverse things, *Eventum tantum* for all events, the ultimate form for all of the forms which remain disjointed in it, but which bring about the resonance and the ramification of their disjunction. The univocity of being merges with the positive use of the disjunctive synthesis which is the highest affirmation. It is the eternal return itself, or — as we have seen in the case of the ideal game — the affirmation of all chance in a single moment, the unique cast for all throws, one Being and only one for all forms and all times, a single insistence for all that exists, a single phantom for all the living, a single voice for every hum of voices and every drop of water in the sea. It would be a mistake to confuse the univocity of being, *qua* being which says itself, with a pseudo-univocity of that of which it is said.

But at the same time, if Being cannot be said without also occurring, if Being is the unique event in which all events communicate with one another, univocity refers both to what occurs and to what is said. Univocity means that it is the same thing which occurs and is said: the attributable to all bodies or states of affairs and the expressible of every proposition. Univocity means the identity of the noematic attribute and that which is expressed linguistically — event and sense. It does not allow being to subsist in the vague state that it used to have in the perspectives of the analogy. Univocity raises and extracts being, in order to distinguish it better from that in which it occurs and from that of which it is said. It wrests being from beings in order to bring it to all of them at once, and to make it fall upon them for all times. Being pure saying and pure event, univocity brings in contact the inner surface of language (insistence) with the outer surface of being (extra-being). Univocal being inheres in language and happens to things; it measures the internal relation of language with the external relation of being. Neither active nor passive, univocal being is neutral. It is *extra-being*, that is, the minimum of being common to the real, the possible, and the impossible. A position in the void of all events in one, an expression in the nonsense of all senses in one, univocal being is the pure form of the Aion, the form of exteriority which relates things and propositions.[1] In short, the univocity of being has three determinations: one single event for all events; one and the same *aliquid* for that which happens and that which is said; and one and the same being for the impossible, the possible, and the real.

Movement and Multiplicities

From *Cinema 1: The Movement-Image,* translated by Hugh Tomlinson and Barbara
Habberjam (Minneapolis: University of Minnesota Press, 1986), pp. 8–11.

AND THIS is Bergson's third thesis, which is also contained in *Creative Evolution.* If
we tried to reduce it to a bare formula, it would be this: not only is the instant an immobile section of movement, but movement is a mobile section of duration, that is,
of the Whole, or of a whole. Which implies that movement expresses something
more profound, which is the change in duration or in the whole. To say that duration is change is part of its definition: it changes and does not stop changing. For
example, matter moves, but does not change. Now movement *expresses* a change in
duration or in the whole. What *is* a problem is on the one hand this expression, and
on the other, this whole-duration identification.

      Movement is a translation in space. Now each time there is a trans-
lation of parts in space, there is also a qualitative change in a whole. Bergson gave
numerous examples of this in *Matter and Memory.* An animal moves, but this is for a
purpose: to feed, migrate, etc. It might be said that movement presupposes a difference of potential, and aims to fill it. If I consider parts or places abstractly—A and
B—I cannot understand the movement which goes from one to the other. But
imagine I am starving at A, and at B there is something to eat. When I have reached
B and had something to eat, what has changed is not only my state, but the state of
the whole which encompassed B, A, and all that was between them. When Achilles
overtakes the tortoise, what changes is the state of the whole which encompassed the

tortoise, Achilles, and the distance between the two. Movement always relates to a change, migration to a seasonal variation. And this is equally true of bodies: the fall of a body presupposes another one which attracts it, and expresses a change in the whole which encompasses them both. If we think of pure atoms, their movements, which testify to a reciprocal action of all the parts of the substance, necessarily express modifications, disturbances, changes of energy in the whole. What Bergson discovers beyond translation is vibration, radiation. Our error lies in believing that it is the any-element-whatevers, external to qualities, which move. But the qualities themselves are pure vibrations which change at the same time as the alleged elements move.[1]

In *Creative Evolution*, Bergson gives an example which is so famous that it no longer surprises us. Putting some sugar in a glass of water, he says that 'I must willy-nilly, wait until the sugar melts'.[2] This is slightly strange, since Bergson seems to have forgotten that stirring with a spoon can help it to dissolve. But what is his main point? That the movement of translation which detaches the sugar particles and suspends them in the water itself expresses a change in the whole, that is, in the content of the glass; a qualitative transition from water which contains a sugar lump to the state of sugared water. If I stir with the spoon, I speed up the movement, but I also change the whole, which now encompasses the spoon, and the accelerated movement continues to express the change of the whole. 'The wholly superficial displacements of masses and molecules studied in physics and chemistry would become, by relation to that inner vital movement (which is transformation and not translation) what the position of a moving object is to the movement of that object in space.'[3] Thus, in his third thesis, Bergson puts forward the following analogy:

$$\frac{immobile\ sections}{movement} = \frac{movement\ as\ mobile\ section}{qualitative\ change}$$

The only difference is this: the ratio on the left-hand side expresses an illusion; and that on the right-hand side, a reality.

Above all, what Bergson wants to say using the glass of sugared water is that my waiting, whatever it be, expresses a duration as mental, spiritual reality. But why does this spiritual duration bear witness, not only for me who wait, but for the whole which changes? According to Bergson the whole is neither given nor giveable (and the error of modern science, like that of ancient science, lay in taking the whole as given, in two different ways). Many philosophers had already said that the whole was neither given nor giveable: they simply concluded from this that the whole was a meaningless notion. Bergson's conclusion is very different: if the whole is not giveable, it is because it is the Open, and because its nature is to change constantly, or to give rise to something new, in short, to endure. 'The duration of the universe must therefore be one with the latitude of creation which can find place in it.'[4] So that each time we find ourselves confronted with a duration, or in a duration, we may conclude that there exists somewhere a whole which is changing, and which is open somewhere. It is widely known that Bergson initially discovered duration as identical to consciousness. But further study of consciousness led him to demonstrate that it only existed in so far as it opened itself upon a whole, by coinciding with the opening up of a whole. Similarly for the living being: in comparing the living being to a whole, or to the whole of the universe, Bergson seems to be reviving the most ancient simile.[5] However, he completely reverses its terms. For, if the living being is a whole and, therefore, comparable to the whole of the universe, this is not because it is a microcosm as closed as the whole is assumed to be, but, on the contrary, because it is open upon a world, and the world, the universe, is itself the Open. 'Wherever anything lives, there is, open somewhere, a register in which time is being inscribed.'[6]

If one had to define the whole, it would be defined by Relation. Relation is not a property of objects, it is always external to its terms. Hence, it is inseparable from the open, and displays a spiritual or mental existence.[7] Relations do not belong to objects, but to the whole, on condition that this is not confused with a closed set of objects.[8] By movement in space, the objects of a set change their respective positions. But, through relations, the whole is transformed or changes qualitatively. We can say of duration itself or of time, that it is the whole of relations.

The whole and the 'wholes' must not be confused with *sets*. Sets are closed, and everything which is closed is artificially closed. Sets are always sets of parts. But a whole is not closed, it is open; and it has no parts except in a very special sense, since it cannot be divided without changing qualitatively at each stage of the division. 'The real whole might well be, we conceive, an indivisible continuity.'[9] The whole is not a closed set, but on the contrary that by virtue of which the set is never absolutely closed, never completely sheltered, that which keeps it open somewhere as if by the finest thread which attaches it to the rest of the universe. The glass of water is indeed a closed set containing the parts, the water, the sugar, perhaps the spoon; but that is not the whole. The whole creates itself, and constantly creates itself in another dimension without parts — like that which carries along the set of one qualitative state to another, like the pure ceaseless becoming which passes through these states. It is in this sense that it is spiritual or mental. 'The glass of water, the sugar, and the process of the sugar's melting in the water are abstractions and ... the

whole within which they have been cut out by my senses and understanding pro-
gresses, it may be, in the manner of a consciousness.'[10] In any case, this artificial division of a set or a closed system is not a pure illusion. It is well founded and, if it is
impossible to break the link of each thing with the whole (this paradoxical link, which
ties it to the open), it can at least be drawn out, stretched to infinity, made finer and
finer. The organisation of matter makes possible the closed systems or the determi-
nate sets of parts; and the deployment of space makes them necessary. But the point
is that the sets are in space, and the whole, the wholes are in duration, are duration
itself, in so far as it does not stop changing. So that the two formulas which corre-
sponded to Bergson's first thesis now take on a much more rigorous status; 'immobile
sections + abstract time' refers to closed sets whose parts are in fact immobile sections, and whose successive states are calculated on an abstract time; while 'real movement → concrete duration' refers to the opening up of a whole which endures, and
whose movements are so many mobile sections crossing the closed systems.

The upshot of this third thesis is that we find ourselves on three
levels: (1) the sets or closed systems which are defined by discernible objects or distinct parts; (2) the movement of translation which is established between these objects and modifies their respective positions; (3) the duration or the whole, a spiritual reality which constantly changes according to its own relations.

Thus in a sense movement has two aspects. On one hand, that
which happens between objects or parts; on the other hand that which expresses the
duration or the whole. The result is that duration, by changing qualitatively, is divided up in objects, and objects, by gaining depth, by losing their contours, are united
in duration. We can therefore say that movement relates the objects of a closed system to open duration, and duration to the objects of the system which it forces to
open up. Movement relates the objects between which it is established to the changing whole which it expresses, and vice versa. Through movement the whole is divided up into objects, and objects are re-united in the whole, and indeed between the
two 'the whole' changes. We can consider the objects or parts of a set as *immobile sections*; but movement is established between these sections, and relates the objects or
parts to the duration of a whole which changes, and thus expresses the changing of
the whole in relation to the objects and is itself a *mobile section* of duration. Now we are
equipped to understand the profound thesis of the first chapter of *Matter and Memory*: (1) there are not only instantaneous images, that is, immobile sections of movement; (2) there are movement-images which are mobile sections of duration; (3)
there are, finally, time-images, that is, duration-images, change-images, relation-im-
ages, volume-images which are beyond movement itself...

Time versus truth

From *Cinema 2: The Time-Image*, translated by Hugh Tomlinson and Robert Galeta

(Minneapolis: University of Minnesota Press, 1989), pp. 130–31. Translation modified.

IF WE take the history of thought, we see that time has always put the notion of truth into crisis. Not that truth varies depending on the epoch. It is not the simple empirical content, it is the form or rather the pure force of time which puts truth into crisis. Since antiquity this crisis has burst out in the paradox of 'contingent futures'. If it is *true* that a naval battle *may* take place tomorrow, how are we to avoid one of the two following consequences;[1] either the impossible proceeds from the possible (since, if the battle takes place, it is no longer possible that it may not take place), or the past is not necessarily true (since the battle could not have taken place).[2] It is easy to regard this paradox as a sophism. It none the less shows the difficulty of conceiving a direct relation between truth and the form of time, and obliges us to keep the true away from the existent, in the eternal or in what imitates the eternal. We have to wait for Leibniz to get the most ingenious, but also the strangest and most convoluted, solution to this paradox. Leibniz says that the naval battle may or may not take place, but that this is not in the same world: it takes place in one world and does not take place in a different world, and these two worlds are possible, but are not 'compossible' with each other.[3] He is thus obliged to forge the wonderful notion of *incompossibility* (very different from contradiction) in order to resolve the paradox while saving truth: according to him, it is not the impossible, but only the incompossible that proceeds from the possible; and the past may be true without being necessarily true. But the crisis of truth thus enjoys a pause rather than a solution. For nothing prevents us from affirming that incompossibles belong to the same world, that incompossible worlds belong to the same universe: 'Fang, for example, has a secret; a stranger calls at his door...Fang can kill the intruder, the intruder can kill Fang, they can both escape, they can both die, and so forth...you arrive at this house, but in one of the possible pasts you are my enemy, in another my friend...'[4] This is Borges's reply to Leibniz: the straight line as force of time, as labyrinth of time, is also the line which forks and keeps on forking, passing through *incompossible presents*, returning to *not-necessarily true pasts*.

A new status of narration follows from this: narration ceases to be truthful, that is, to claim to be true, and becomes fundamentally falsifying. This is not at all a case of 'each has its own truth', a variability of content. It is a power of the false which replaces and supersedes the form of the true, because it poses the simultaneity of incompossible presents, or the coexistence of not-necessarily true pasts. Crystalline description was already reaching the indiscernibility of the real and the imaginary, but the falsifying narration which corresponds to it goes a step further and poses inexplicable differences in the present and alternatives which are undecidable between true and false in the past. The truthful man dies, every model of truth collapses, in favour of the new narration. We have not mentioned the author who is essential in this regard: it is Nietzsche, who, under the name of 'will to power', substitutes the power of the false for the form of the true, and resolves the crisis of truth, wanting to settle it once and for all, but, in opposition to Leibniz, in favour of the false and its artistic, creative power...

The Thought of the Outside

From *Foucault,* translated by Seán Hand (Minneapolis: University of Minnesota Press, 1988), pp. 116–19. Translation modified.

BUT IF it is true that the conditions are no more general or constant than the conditioned element, it is none the less the conditions that interest Foucault. This is why he calls his work historical research and not the work of a historian. He does not write a history of mentalities but of the conditions governing everything that has a mental existence, namely statements and the system of language. He does not write a history of behaviour but of the conditions governing everything that has a visible existence, namely a system of light. He does not write a history of institutions but of the conditions governing their integration of differential relations between forces, at the limits of a social field. He does not write a history of private life but of the conditions governing the way in which the relation to oneself constitutes a private life. He does not write a history of subjects but of processes of subjectivation, governed by the foldings operating in the ontological as much as the social field.[1] In truth, one thing haunts Foucault—thought. The question: 'What does thinking signify? What is called thinking?' is the arrow first fired by Heidegger and then again by Foucault. He writes a history, but a history of thought as such. To think means to experiment and to problematize. Knowledge, power and the self are the triple root of a problematization of thought. In the field of knowledge as problem, thinking is first of all seeing and speaking, but thinking is carried out in the space between the two, in the interstice or disjunction between seeing and speaking. On each occasion it invents the intertwining, firing an arrow from the one towards the target of the other, creating a flash of light in the midst of words, or unleashing a cry in the midst of visible things. Thinking makes both seeing and speaking attain their individual limits, such that the two are the common limit that both separates and links them.

On top of this, in the field of power as problem, thinking involves the transmission of singularities: it is a dice-throw. What the dice-throw expresses is that thinking always comes from the outside (that outside which was already engulfed in the interstice or which constituted the common limit). Thinking is neither innate nor acquired. It is not the innate exercise of a faculty, but neither is it a learning process constituted in the external world. Artaud contrasted the innate and the acquired with the "genital", the genitality of thought as such, a thought which comes from an outside that is farther away than any external world, and hence closer than any internal world. Must this outside be called Chance?[2] The dice-throw does in fact express the simplest possible power- or force-relation, the one established between singularities arrived at by chance (the numbers on the different faces).

The relations between forces, as Foucault understands them, concern not only human beings but the elements, the letters of the alphabet, which group either fortuitously or according to certain laws of attraction and frequency dictated by a particular language. Chance applies only to the first throw; while the second throw perhaps operates under conditions that are partially determined by the first, as in a Markov chain, where we have a succession of partial re-concatenations. This is the outside: the line that continually re-concatenates fortuitous selections in mixtures of chance and dependency. Consequently, thinking here takes on new figures: fortuitously selecting singularities, re-concatenating the selections; and on each occasion inventing the series that extend from the neighbourhood of a singularity to the neighbourhood of another. There are all sorts of singularities which have all come from outside: singularities of power, caught up in the relations between forces; singularities of resistance, which pave the way for change; and even *wild* singularities which remain suspended outside, without entering into relations or allowing themselves to be integrated (only here does 'wild' take on a meaning, not as an experience but as that which cannot yet be absorbed into experience).[3]

All these determinations of thought are already original figures of the action of thought. And for a long time Foucault did not believe that thought could be anything else. How could thought invent a morality, since thought can find nothing in itself except that outside from which it comes and which resides in it as "the unthought"? That *Fiat!* which destroys any imperative in advance.[4] However,

Foucault senses the emergence of a strange final figure: if the outside, farther away than any external world, is also closer than any internal world, is this not a sign that thought affects itself, by discovering the outside to be its own unthought element?

> It cannot discover the unthought [...] without immediately bringing the unthought nearer to itself—or even, perhaps, without pushing it further away, and in any case without causing man's own being to undergo a change by that very fact, since it is deployed in the distance between them.[5]

This auto-affection, this conversion of far and near, will assume more and more importance by constructing an *inside-space* that will be completely co-present with the outside-space on the line of the fold. The problematical unthought gives way to a thinking being who problematizes himself, as an ethical subject (in Artaud this is the 'innate genital'; in Foucault it is the meeting between self and sexuality). To think is to fold, to double the outside with a coextensive inside. The general topology of thought, which had already begun 'in the neighbourhood' of the singularities, now comes to completion in the folding of the outside into the inside: 'in the interior of the exterior and inversely', as *Madness and Civilization* put it. We have shown how any organization (differentiation and integration) presupposed the primary topological structure of an absolute outside and inside that induces relative intermediary exteriorities and interiorities: the entire inside-space is topologically in contact with the outside-space, independently of distance, and on the limits of a 'living'; and this carnal or vital topology, far from showing up in space, frees a time that condenses the past in the inside, brings about the future in the outside, and brings the two into confrontation at the limit of the living present.[6]

Notes

Translator's Preface: Portraiture in Philosophy, or Shifting Perspectives

1. Gilles Deleuze, *Foucault*, trans. Seán Hand (Minneapolis: University of Minnesota Press, 1988).

2. Gilles Deleuze, "Life as a Work of Art," in *Negotiations 1972–1990*, trans. Martin Joughin (New York: Columbia University Press, 1995). I have however, referred to the French edition of this book; thus all cited phrases are in my own translation. One might note that the other interviews bearing on Foucault in *Negotiations* are also pertinent in this context.

3. Gilles Deleuze and Félix Guattari, *What Is Philosophy?*, trans. Hugh Tomlinson and Graham Burchell (New York: Columbia University Press, 1994). Originally published as *Qu'est-ce que la philosophie?* (Paris: Minuit, 1991).

4. Alain Badiou *Manifesto for Philosophy*, trans. Norman Madarasz (Albany: State University of New York Press, 1999). Originally published as *Manifeste pour la philosophie* (Paris: Seuil, 1989). The two essays published with the translation of *Manifesto*, "The (Re)turn of Philosophy Itself" and "Definition of Philosophy," were originally published in *Conditions* (Paris: Seuil, 1992).

5. Jean-Jacques Leclercle, "Cantor, Lacan, Mao, Beckett, *même combat*: The Philosophy of Alain Badiou," in *Radical Philosophy* (January–February 1999): 6–13;

Lauren Sedofsky, "Being by Numbers," an interview with Alain Badiou, *Artforum* (October 1994): 84–124.

6. Alain Badiou, *L'Etre et l'événement* (Paris: Seuil, 1988).

7. The remarks by Lacoue-Labarthe and Lyotard were made in the framework of a discussion organized at the Collège international de philosophie in Paris and published in *Le Cahier du collège international de philosophie* (Paris: Osiris, 1989); Janicaud's statement comes from his survey of contemporary French philosophy in Raymond Klibansky and David Pears, eds., *La Philosophie en Europe* (Paris: Gallimard/UNESCO, 1993).

8. Other than *L'Etre et l'événement*, this very succinct presentation of Badiou's thought draws on *Manifeste pour la philosophie* and *Conditions*.

9. Alain Badiou, "Gilles Deleuze, *The Fold: Leibniz and the Baroque*," trans. T. Sowley, in Constantin V. Boundas and Dorothea Olkowski, eds., *Gilles Deleuze and the Theater of Philosophy* (New York and London: Routledge, 1994), pp. 51–69. Originally published as "Gilles Deleuze, *Le Pli. Leibniz et le Baroque*," in *Annuaire philosophique 1988–1989* (Paris: Seuil, 1989), pp. 161–84.

10. Deleuze and Guattari, *What Is Philosophy?*, pp. 151–53.

11. This characterization of the two opposing paradigms of the multiple is Badiou's own, as presented both in his article on *The Fold* and in the introductory chapter of the present book. Badiou elaborates what he understands by Deleuze's adherence to a vital or "animal" paradigm in the following terms: "The multiple as a large animal made up of animals, the organic respiration inherent to one's own organicity, the multiple as *living tissue*, which folds as if under the effect of its organic expandings and contractings, in perfect contradiction with the Cartesian concept of extension as punctual and regulated by the shock: Deleuze's philosophy is the capture of a life that is both total and divergent. No wonder he pays tribute to Leibniz, who upholds, more than any other philosopher, 'the assertion of one sole and same world, and of the infinite difference and variety found in this world' " ("Gilles Deleuze, *The Fold*," p. 55).

12. Deleuze and Guattari, *What Is Philosophy?*, p. 152. In sum, for Deleuze, however interesting Badiou's philosophical undertaking may be (and Deleuze and Guattari do describe it as a contemporary undertaking of particular interest), insofar as it is organized around the hypothesis of "any multiplicity whatever" in accordance with the paradigm of a set-theoreticism that "even mathematics has had enough of," Badiou's conceptualization not only completely fails to found a theory of multiplicities, but is positioned on the level of scientific functions and not on that of philosophical concepts.

13. The series, titled "Coup double," adopts a format whereby a critical commentary is followed by a selection of texts from the author under discussion. Badiou's essay on Beckett, *Beckett. L'Increvable désir*, was published in 1995.

14. Bernard Sichère, "Badiou lit Deleuze," *Critique*, no. 605 (October 1997): 722.

15. Jean-Clet Martin, *Variations. La Philosophie de Gilles Deleuze* (Paris: Payot and Rivages, 1993). Martin recounted this anecdote concerning Badiou's description of his book on the occasion of a roundtable organized by the Collège international de philosophie in February 1998.

16. Need one remark here that the metaphysical tradition is not one great homogeneous bloc?

17. As Arnaud Villani remarks in his article (directed against Badiou's interpretation of this metaphysics) "La métaphysique de Deleuze," *Futur Antérieur*, no. 43 (1998): 55–70. See equally: Arnaud Villani, *La Guêpe et l'orchidée. Essai sur* Gilles Deleuze (Paris: Belin, 1999), p. 35.

18. Badiou cites this formula addressed to him by Deleuze in a chapter dealing with "Deleuze's vitalist ontology" in his recent book *Court traité d'ontologie transitoire* (Paris: Seuil, 1998), p. 62.

19. See Martin Heidegger, *Kant and the Problem of Metaphysics* (1929), trans. Richard Taft, (Bloomington: Indiana University Press, 1997), pp. 140–41 and Heidegger's preface to the fourth edition, p. xviii.

20. This characterization of Deleuze's interventions in the history of philosophy is found in his letter to Michel Cressole, in *Negotiations 1972–1990*; Badiou's remarks were made on the occasion of the discussion already mentioned, with Jean-Clet Martin and Françoise Proust, organized by the Collège international de philosophie in February 1998.

21. The references here are the following: *Difference and Repetition*, trans. Paul Patton (New York: Columbia University Press, 1994), and *The Logic of Sense*, trans. Mark Lester with Charles Stivale (New York: Columbia University Press, 1990).

22. See Martin Heidegger, *Nietzsche*, trans. David Farrell Krell (London: Routledge and Kegan Paul, 1981), esp. vol. 1, pp. 200 ff. ("Nietzsche's Overturning of Platonism").

23. André Lalande, *Vocabulaire technique et critique de la philosophie* (Paris: Presses Universitaires de France, 1926).

24. This dictionary, *Les Notions philosophiques* (edited by Sylvain Auroux and published in 1990), forms part of the *Encyclopédie philosophique universelle* (Paris: Presses Universitaires de France).

25. By way of engaging a dialogue on the translation of Deleuze, I would note here that, in my opinion, the translation of *Difference and Repetition* should have included some indication, each time that the word "ground" appears in the text, as to which French term is involved. In failing to differentiate in any way whatsoever between the two distinct French words translated as "ground," the English translation loses a nuance of meaning that is vital to Deleuze's text and thus, at times, contains passages that are more or less incomprehensible (as, for example, the passage found on pp. 274–75, in which the proliferation of "grounds," rendering at times *fondement*, at times *fond*, makes it impossible to follow coherently Deleuze's exposition of the way in which the *fondement*, understood as "the operation of logos, or of sufficient reason," serves as the "foundation" for the forms of representation but, at the same time, is interwoven, as it were, with the *fond* or "ground" into which it plunges). That said, I obviously do not wish to minimize the problems that Deleuze's text poses for the translator. And Paul Patton does consider such problems in his preface. Unfortunately, however, he accentuates the distinction between *fondation* (rendered as "foundation") and *fondement* ("ground")—which, in my eyes, is not all that important (*fondation* having the sense of the operation of founding, or, in other words, of encompassing the process of selection that follows from the determination of the *fondement*)—while completely ignoring the important distinction between *fondement* and *fond*.

26. Gilles Deleuze, *Cinema 1: The Movement-Image*, trans. Hugh Tomlinson and Barbara Habberjam (Minneapolis: University of Minnesota Press, 1986).

27. See George Santayana, *Three Philosophical Poets* [1910] (New York: Doubleday Anchor Books, 1953), p. 27.

28. Although I have referred to the French edition of Deleuze's text, English-language readers can refer to *Bergsonism*, trans. Hugh Tomlinson and Barbara Habberjam (New York: Zone Books, 1988), chapter 5.

29. Deleuze gives a long note dealing with Markov chains and with his understanding of reconcatenation as referring to partially dependent successive selections or semifortuitous concatenations in *Cinema 2: The Time-Image*, trans. Hugh Tomlinson and Robert Galeta (Minneapolis: University of Minnesota Press, 1989), pp. 213 and 303 n. 36.

30. In her translation of Heidegger's *Being and Time* (Albany: State University of New York Press, 1996), Joan Stambaugh uses the lowercase for "being" to avoid any substantivization of the word; as she states in her Translator's Preface, capitalizing "being" risks implying — directly counter to Heidegger's understanding of the word — that it is some kind of Super Thing or transcendent being.

Introduction

1. Ecole normale supérieure: There exist four university-level colleges of this type in France, which prepare students for careers in academia and research. The Ecole situated in Paris's Latin Quarter (rue d'Ulm), which Badiou attended, is the oldest and most venerable of these extremely prestigious institutions and has historically functioned as a veritable nurturing ground for the elite of French intelligentsia. Indeed, Deleuze is "singular" among French philosophers in *not* having studied there. [*Trans.*]

2. The Univerity of Vincennes was created in the wake of May 1968, as an "experimental center" where the new principles that were supposed to govern henceforth university education — namely, autonomy, multidisciplinarity, and student participation — were to be enacted exemplarily. Badious was a member of the teaching staff from the beginning, have been solicited by foucault, who was at that moment in charge of the recruiting committee for philosophy — and who subsequently became head of the philosophy department. Deleuze had also been solicited by foucault at the inception of Vincennes, but ill heath prevented him from joining the department until two years later, when foucault had already left and François Châtelet had taken over as head of the department. In 1978, the building of Vincennes were razed adn the faculty was transferred to Saint-Denis, a northern suburb of Paris. [*Trans.*]

3. François Regnault, like Alain Badiou, was invited to teach at Vincennes by Foucault. Like Badiou equally, he had been part of the group Cahiers de l'analyse, and "influenced" by Althusser and Lacan while a student at the Ecole normale. Badiou mentions Regnault in a note of *L'Etre et l'événement* (see note 9) as one of those with whose work — which centers on theater, "that superior art," as Badiou puts it, in citing Mallarmé — he recognizes a "proximity."

Jean Borreil (1938–93), who taught at Vincennes from 1971 on, was particularly interested in the relation between painting and philosophy. It does not seem superfluous to note here that Jacques Rancière, in his preface to a posthumous compilation of Borreil's essays, describes the figure of the "artist-king" that Borreil explored in his book of the same name (*L'Artiste-Roi* [Paris: Aubier, 1989]) as having opened up a "Platonism against Plato," which may be situated between "the 'reascent of simulacra' of which Gilles Deleuze speaks and Alain Badiou's 'Platonism of the multiple'" (Jean Borreil, *La Raison nomade* [Paris: Payot, 1993], p. 15). An essay by Alain Badiou, "Jean Borreil: le style d'une pensée," is included in a book of homages to Borreil, *Jean Borreil: la raison de l'autre* (Paris: Harmattan, 1995). [*Trans.*]

4. Alain Badiou, with François Balmès, *De l'idéologie* (Paris: Maspero, 1976). [*Trans.*]

5. Badiou is referring to the text that appeared in the newspaper *Le Monde*, June 19–20, 1977, p. 19: "Gilles Deleuze contre les 'nouveaux philosophes'" (Gilles Deleuze against the "New Philosophers"). This text was reprinted, under the title "A propos des nouveaux philosophes et d'un problème plus général," in *Minuit*, suppl., no. 24, June 1977. [*Trans.*]

6. Alain Badiou *Théorie du sujet* (Paris: Seuil, 1982). [*Trans.*]

7. Jean-François Lyotard, *The Differend*, trans. Georges Van Den Abbeele (Minneapolis: University of Minnesota Press, 1988). Originally published as *Le Différend* (Paris: Minuit, 1983). [*Trans.*]

8. Alain Badiou, "Custos, Quid Noctis?" *Critique*, no. 450 (November 1984): 851–63. [*Trans.*]

9. Alain Badiou, *L'étre et l'événement* (Being and event) (Paris: Seuil, 1988). In the introduction to this book of a rare ambition, Badiou writes: "The initial thesis of my undertaking . . . is the following: the science of being qua being *exists* since the Greeks, for such is the status and sense that accrue to mathematics. But it is only today that we have the means to *know* this. It follows from this thesis that philosophy does not have ontology for its center — for ontology exists as an exact and distinct discipline — but that it *circulates* between ontology, the modern theories of the subject, and its own history." And he goes on to state his conviction that "mathematics inscribes that which, of being as such, can be pronounced in the field of a pure theory of the Multiple. The entire history of rational thought [becomes clear once one adopts] the hypothesis that the exceptional severity of the law governing mathematics — which can thus in no way be reduced to game without an object— is a function of mathematics' being bound to the task of upholding ontological discourse" (pp. 9, 10–11). [*Trans.*]

10. The text by Wahl, titled "Le soustractif" (The substractive), devotes its first nineteen pages to the confrontation between Deleuze and Badiou, in declaring that it is precisely by means of such a confrontation— given as much the points of convergence as those of opposition between the philosophies of the two thinkers— that the kernel of Badiou's thought can be made apparent (*Conditions* [Paris: Seuil, 1992], pp. 9–54. [*Trans.*]

11. The "report" by Éric Alliez was, effectively, written at the request of the board dealing with cultural relations, within the French Ministry of Foreign Affairs, and appeared in 1994, along with two other texts (by Christian Descamps and Jocelyn Benoist, respectively), in a document published by the ministry: *Philosophie contemporaine en France* (Paris: adpf, 1994). Alliez's text was subsequently republished, in a revised and expanded form, under the title *De l'impossibilité de la phénoménologie. Sur la philosophie française contemporaine* (Paris: Vrin, 1995). For the discussion of Badiou's work, see pp. 81–87. [*Trans.*]

12. *Annuaire philosophique* was the title of an annual collection of extensive and detailed critical reviews of selected philosophical texts that had been published during the preceding academic year. This "philosophical annual" was published by Seuil.

Deleuze's book *Le Pli: Leibniz et le baroque* (*The Fold: Leibniz and the Baroque*, trans. Tom Conley [Minneapolis: University of Minnesota Press, 1993] was published in 1988 (Paris: Minuit). Badiou's article thus appeared in the *Annuaire philosophique* covering the year 1988–89 (pp. 161–84). For the English translation of Badiou's text, see "Gilles Deleuze, *The Fold: Leibniz and the Baroque*," trans. Thelma Sowley, in Constantin V. Boundas, and Dorothea Olkowski, eds., *Gilles Deleuze and the Theater of Philosophy* (New York and London: Routledge, 1994), pp. 51–69. [*Trans.*]

13. Gilles Deleuze and Félix Guattari, *What Is Philosophy?*, trans. Hugh Tomlinson and Graham Burchell (New York: Columbia University Press, 1994). Originally published as *Qu'est-ce que la philosophie?* (Paris: Minuit, 1991). [*Trans.*]

14. The Collège international de philosophie is an autonomous educational and research institution, founded in 1983, that offers researchers the possibility to present their work, while the general public is offered open access to a large range of seminars and colloquiums. Badiou's seminars take place at the Collège in the framework of an agreement with the University of Vincennes-Saint-Denis. The four seminars devoted to *What Is Philosophy?* were given from October 23 to December 4, 1991. [*Trans.*]

15. *Tombeau:* This term usually refers to a literary or musical composition written to honor the memory of someone renowned. Badiou's use of the term here, however, bears the inflection that Mallarmé was to give to it as an "incarnation" of the deceased in a work that thus ensures the latter's survival. For Mallarmé—whose *tombeaux* are consecrated to Poe, Baudelaire, Verlaine, and Théophile Gautier (as well as to his son, Anatole)— this inflection takes its full meaning when the person so honored is a poet; for not only is the best way to honor a poet's memory to erect a *literary* monument (see "The Tomb of Edgar on Poe," line 10f.) but it is, above all, by the means of their own work that poets continue to live on. Of course, the poet, for Mallarmé, is not simply someone who "writes"; for, far from being merely a "work of art," the poem is that which must succeed religion as the means by which humanity attains its highest point. But be that as it may, in the case of Badiou's use of the term *tombeau*, it is, indeed, in his words, his work, that the *philosopher*, Gilles Deleuze, lives on. We might add that the short text that Badiou wrote for the pages devoted to Deleuze, shortly after his death, by the newspaper *Le Monde*, was titled "Pour un tombeau" (*Le Monde*, Literary Supplement, November 10, 1995, p. x). [*Trans.*]

1. Which Deleuze?

1. The English translation of Deleuze's text gives, in fact, "petrified" instead of "purified." This is quite simply an error. [*Trans.*]

2. *destined to repetition:* The French syntagm that I have translated in this way employs the term *destination*, which is equally found in the preceding paragraph ("the destination . . . that is thought's own"); as regards this term, readers are referred to chapter 2, translator's note 2. [*Trans.*]

2. Univocity of Being and Multiplicity of Names

1. *being of beings:* For readers surprised to find the question of "the being of beings" cast entirely in lowercase letters, I reiterate here that I have scrupulously respected Badiou's use of capitalization and lowercase, and hence have only capitalized the word "being" where *être* is capitalized in the original text. I remind readers, moreover, that, in her recent translation of Heidegger's *Being and Time* (New York: State University of New York Press, 1996), Joan Stambaugh has chosen not to capitalize the term "being" to avoid any implication of substantivization. [*Trans.*]

2. *finality:* Both this word and the word "destiny" that appears earlier in the paragraph are translations of the French *destination*. It is important to note that *destination*, along with *destin*, is a standard rendering in French translations of Heidegger's texts of the German term *Geschick* (as Heidegger uses it, for example, in the expression *Seingeschick*: the *"sending," "mittence," "mission,"* or *"destiny" of being*, to proffer but some of the proposed translations in English). Admittedly, given the particularly complex and convoluted context characterizing the translation of Heidegger in France, both *destination* and *destin* have also been proposed as renderings for other, quite distinct terms in Heidegger's vocabulary: indeed, Emmanuel Martineau, in his translation of *Sein und Zeit* (*Etre et Temps* [Paris: Authentica, 1985]), reserves *destin* for *Schicksal* (rendered as "fate" in John Macquarrie and Edward Robinson's translation of *Being and Time* [Oxford: Basil Blackwell, 1980]) — which is precisely differentiated, in paragraph 74 of Heidegger's text, from *Geschick* ("destiny" in Macquarrie and Robinson's translation, and rendered by Martineau as *co-destin*). At the same time, Martineau reserves *destination* for the translation of *Hingehören*, which has been rendered in English as "belonging-somewhere." Yet such complications may be put aside here, for, in Alain Badiou's use of the terms *destination* and *destin*, as the author confirmed when consulted on these points, the reference — when reference there is — is principally to *Geschick* (and not to *Schicksal*, and even less to *Hingehören*). On the other hand, however, Badiou's use of the term *destination* does not exclusively refer to the specific context of Heidegger's use of *Geschick*, however marked it may be by a Heideggerian resonance. For these reasons, the translations of *destination* in this text vary (with the French signaled in notes, excepting the cases when it has been rendered by its English cognate "destination"), while *destin* has been systematically translated as "destiny." Finally, the term *destinal* — where the Heideggerian reference is unmistakable — has been rendered as "destining." [*Trans.*]

3. *historical*: The French here is *historial* — an "archaic" word of the French language, which has, since the translation proposed in 1938 by Henri Corbin of chapter 5 of Heidegger's *Sein und Zeit*, constituted the standard rendering in French of *geschichtlich*, in its sharp distinction from *historisch*. Whereas *historisch* designates the configuration of chronological "facts" and relations and is thus correlated to what Heidegger calls a "science of history" (*Historie*), *geschichtlich* is a word closely related to *geschicklich* (from the substantive *Geschick*, discussed in the preceding note) and thus may be said to designate that "which constitutes our lot and where it is a question of our destiny." Macquarrie and Robinson, in their translation of *Being and Time*, render *geschichtlich* by "historical" and *historische* by "historic." It is thus in conformity with this translation that *historial* is rendered here as "historical"; however, rather than render the French adjective *historique* (which is normally translated as "historical") as "historic," and thus introduce — in our opinion — an unwarranted semantic tension in Badiou's use of this common adjective and in the reader's reception of the text, I have preferred to signal by notes the two occasions on which Badiou uses *historial*. [*Trans.*]

4. Aristotle, *Metaphysics*, G, II, 1003 a 33. The translation proposed by Hugh Tredennick (Loeb Classical Library [Cambridge: Harvard University Press (1933) 1989]) is: "The term 'being' is used in various senses." [*Trans.*]

5. "Being" (*Etre*) has been capitalized in conformity with the manner that this sentence is transcribed in Badiou's text: that is, although *être* is written with a lowercase "e" in Deleuze's text, the word appears with a capital letter in the quotation. [*Trans.*]

6. This clause is emphasized in Deleuze's text. [Trans.]

7. Same remark as note 5 above. [*Trans.*]

8. Same remark as note 5 above. [*Trans.*]

9. Same remark as note 5 above. [*Trans.*]

3. Method

1. "Being" (*Etre*) has been capitalized in conformity with the manner that this sentence is transcribed in Badiou's text: that is, although *être* is written with a lowercase "e" in Deleuze's text. [*Trans.*]

2. Same remark as note 1 above. [*Trans.*]

3. *obscure ground:* The French word that is rendered (both here and immediately below) by "ground" is *fond*. This term is discussed both in the Translator's Preface and in chapter 4, translator's note 1. [*Trans.*]

4. Readers should keep in mind that "whole" renders the French *tout*, which has, up to this point of Badiou's text, been translated as "all": hence "the One-All" is the translation of *l'Un-Tout*. Although readers should refer to the Translator's Preface for the explication of this dual rendering of the term *tout*, I would remind them that, in the context of the "case-Bergson," the translation of *tout* by "whole" conforms to the English translations of Bergson's texts. [*Trans.*]

5. *enjoyment* (rendering the French *jouissance*): Although I would follow the remarks of Martin Joughin (in a note to his translation of Deleuze's *Expressionism in Philosophy: Spinoza* [New York: Zone Books, 1990], p. 412), when he upholds the distinction between "Spinozist 'joy' in general" and the "beatific joy or *jouissance* — the full possession of joy in a sort of dispossession of oneself" that is designated by the word "beatitude" — I do not feel that the use of the word "enjoyment" here risks engendering any confusion with Spinoza's "joy" in general. I would add, moreover, that the impossibility of distinguishing whether the expression "enjoyment of the Impersonal" employs an "objective" or "subjective" complement renders "one's possession of joy in a sort of dispossession" indiscernible from the "self-enjoyment of the Impersonal." [*Trans.*]

4. The Virtual

1. *fond:* Derived from the Latin *fundus* ("bottom" and "piece of land"), this root is found, for example, in the series of French words *fonder* ("to found" or "to ground"), *fondement* ("foundation" or "ground"), *s'effondrer* ("to founder," "to collapse," or "to cave in"), *fondation* ("foundation"), *fondamental* ("fundamental"). Of course, the English "found" is cognate with *fond*, while "ground" is cognate with the German *Grund* (both deriving from the Germanic *grunduz*). Having integrated both Latin and German roots, the English language thus offers us two series of cognates by which to translate the series of cognates of *fond* (although, interesting enough, it is the series cognate with "ground" or words derived from other Germanic roots that, in general, best render the different senses of the word *fond* itself: "ground," "background," "bottom," "back"—with the exception of "basis" and the anatomical term "fundus"). Conversely, the French language, having developed directly from Latin, must resort precisely to *fond* or *fondement* in order to translate the German *Grund*. Although I have translated both *fond* and *fondement* by "ground" (with the series of cognates on which Deleuze plays in the passage that Badiou goes on to quote from *The Logic of Sense* being, accordingly, rendered by cognates of "ground" rather than of "found"), I would remind the reader that these terms are not strictly identical in the use that Deleuze himself makes of them. For this reason (discussed in greater detail in the Translator's Preface), wherever "ground" translates *fond* rather than *fondement*, the French has been given in the text. [*Trans.*]

2. Both the English "there is" and the French *il y a* (which the former renders here) are standard ways of translating the German *es gibt* as Heidegger uses it in the expressions—distinguished from prepositional statements—*Es gibt Sein* ("It gives being") or *Es gibt Zeit* ("It gives time"). Accordingly, in the context of this definition of the virtual as absolute "givenness"—or, more literally, absolute "giving"—readers should be aware that the *il y a* in Badiou's text could equally be translated as "it gives," in conformity with certain translations of the Heideggerian formulation. [*Trans.*]

3. *Actual terms never resemble the virtuality they actualize:* This sentence does not, in fact, figure in the English translation of *Difference and Repetition*. The translator has inadvertently omitted a couple of lines of Deleuze's text, linking the beginning of the sentence (or more precisely, the clause) reproduced here with the end of the sentence's final clause two lines below. The (truncated) English text thus gives: "Actual terms never resemble the singularities they incarnate." It should, however, read as follows: "Actual terms never resemble the virtuality they actualize: the qualities and species no more resemble the differential relations they incarnate than the parts resemble the singularities that they incarnate." Cf. *Différence et répétition*, p. 273, and the English translation, p. 212. [*Trans.*]

4. *that to which everything is destined:* The French clause that has been rendered in this way employs the noun

destination, which was discussed in chapter 2, translator's note 2. [*Trans.*]

5. *ignorantiae asylum:* See *Ethics*, part 1, Appendix, where Spinoza describes those who uphold the doctrine of final causes, instead of seeking a scientific explanation for phenomena, as taking refuge in divine will—that "asylum of ignorance." [*Trans.*]

5. Time and Truth

1. See the Introduction, note 9. [*Trans.*]

2. The expression "forms-of-the-true" renders the French *formes-vraies*, which one might have expected to be translated as "true-forms." However, this latter translation not only fundamentally insinuates an adjectival value to the word "true" (whereas, were it not for the fact that Badiou tends to avoid the substantive *vérité*, a possible translation might have been "truth-forms"), but Badiou goes on to employ the expression *formes du vrai* ("forms of the true") in the following paragraph (just as he has, in his preceding paragraph, spoken of "the actual forms of Being-true [*l'Etre-vrai*]"). As a general rule, moreover, in the French language, the use of hyphenated compounds marks precisely that the elements so grouped stand in a different syntactical relationship or category than that characterizing their nonhyphenated collocation; in the case of *formes-vraies*, for example, *vraies* is taken up in a noun-phase and released from its adjectival function (although still bearing the lexical marks of this function), while at the same time the genitive relationship present in the expression *formes du vrai* is suppressed. Indeed, Badiou expressly advocates, when discussing later on the term *pensée du dehors* (in the sense of "thought *of* the outside"), the use of a hyphenated compound as a way of avoiding any such genitive—or, in the occurrence, intentional—relationship, as the reader will discover in chapter 7 of this book. Although it is unfortunate that the English expression "forms-of-the-true" (as well as the expression "affirmation-of-the-true"—*affirmation-vraie*—which appears in the text immediately below) formally retains such a relationship, the reader should understand the hyphenated structure as posing all its terms on the same "level" or the same "plane." [*Trans.*]

3. See Plato, *Timaeus*, 37d. [*Trans.*]

4. The precise wording of Hegel's formula, found in the *Phenomenology of Spirit*, is: "Time is the Notion itself, which is there" (trans. A. V. Miller [Oxford: Oxford University Press, 1977], p. 487); or, in the rendering given by John Macquarrie and Edward Robinson in their translation of Heidegger's *Being and Time* (Oxford: Basil Blackwell, 1980): "*time* is the *concept* itself, which is there" (p. 485). Both these translations are in strict conformity with the German text: "Die *Zeit* ist der *Begriff* selbst, der *da ist*" (Hegel, *Phänomenologie des*

Geistes, in *Werke*, vol. 2, p. 604). However, in his quotation of this formula in French—"le temps est l'être-là du Concept"—Badiou renders it as though the da ist ("which *is there*," or, in French, "qui *est là*") of the German text is given in the nominal form *Dasein* (i.e., "being-there" = "être-là"). One might note, in this respect, that the French language is marked by a strong tendency to nominalization of this sort. [*Trans.*]

5. *presentation*: Badiou defines this term, in *L'être et l'événement* (Paris: Seuil, 1988), as "the being-multiple as effectively deployed" (p. 555). As such, "presentation" is exchangeable with "inconsistent multiplicity": the point here being that what makes the multiple consistent is the "operation of the one," which Badiou names "the count-as-one." In the same book, he notes that the presentation as pure multiple is a major theme of our epoch, linked principally with the names of Gilles Deleuze and Jean-François Lyotard. He also specifies that his use of "presentation" is especially indebted to Lyotard's use of the term (see pp. 522–23, and 31f.). [*Trans.*]

6. *situation*: Badiou defines this term as "any consistent multiplicity that is presented." This means that the situation entails, therefore, not only a multiple—whatever its terms may be—but also "an operator of the count-as-one, which is proper to it," or, in other words, a "structure," defined as that which prescribes, for a presented multiplicity, the regime of the "count-as-one" (cf. *L'Etre et l'événement*, pp. 557, 32). Elsewhere (in an interview with Lauren Sedofsky, "Being by Numbers," *Artforum* (October 1994), Badiou describes less formally the situation as "an ordinary multiple, a multiple that is obviously infinite because all situations in reality are infinite. It can be a historical, political, artistic, or mathematic situation; it can even be a subjective situation. I take situation in an exceptionally open sense, and to capture that openness I say it's a multiplicity" (p. 87). See equally note 5 above and chapter 7, note 4. [*Trans.*]

6. Eternal Return and Chance

1. *every truth is a fidelity*: Badiou elaborates on this statement in his article "On a Finally Objectless Subject" (*Topoi* [1988]; trans. Bruce Fink) in the following terms: "The process of a truth is fidelity (to the event), i.e., the evaluation, using a specific operator (that of fidelity), of the degree of connection between the terms of the situation and the supernumerary name of the event" (p. 94). In sum, as Badiou states in the "meditation" consecrated to the fidelity in *L'Etre et l'événement* (Paris: Seuil, 1988), "a fidelity" is "the apparatus that separates, in the ensemble of presented multiples, those that depend on an event. Being faithful consists in assembling and in distinguishing a legitimate becoming from what is merely fortuitous" (p. 257). [*Trans.*]

2. See Herman Melville, "Bartleby," in *The Piazza Tales* (1856); and Gilles Deleuze, "Bartleby, or the Formula,"

in *Essays Critical and Clinical*, trans. Daniel W. Smith and Michael A. Greco (Minneapolis: University of Minnesota Press, 1997). [*Trans.*]

3. See Samuel Beckett, *The Unnamable*, trans. from the French by the author (New York: Grove Press, 1958), p. 179; and, among other references, Deleuze's "The Exhausted," trans. Anthony Uhlmann, *Substance* 24:3 (1995). As mentioned in the Translator's Preface, Alain Badiou has himself written—in addition to a number of essays—a book on Beckett (Paris: Hachette, 1995). One might note, in this context, that the third chapter of this book is titled "The Methodical Ascesis." [*Trans.*]

4. See Plato, *Timaeus*, 48a 6–7. [*Trans.*]

5. The word "differences" that Badiou has inserted in brackets in this quotation replaces the word "series" (specified as divergent) in Deleuze's text. [*Trans.*]

6. The emphasis is Deleuze's, although this has not been respected in the English translation of *Difference and Repetition*. [*Trans.*]

7. *chao-errancy*: The French term here, *chao-errance*, has been rendered in the English translation of *The Logic of Sense* as "chao-odyssey" (p. 264). I have preferred to retain the "homophony" of the opposition "coherency" and "chao-errancy," in presuming that the readers will understand that "errancy" is not to be understood as referring to a state of "error." [*Trans.*]

7. The Outside and the Fold

1. Parmenides' Fragment 5 (in Diels's classification) may be translated in more ways than one; for example, the translation given in G. S. Kirk, J. E. Raven, and M. Schofield, *The Presocratic Philosophers* (Cambridge: Cambridge University Press, 1983), is as follows: "For the same thing is there both to be thought of and to be" (p. 246 n. 2), whereas the most usual version is: "For thinking and being are the same." Badiou, for his part, cites this fragment in a translation that conforms to that by Jean Beaufret (*Le Poème de Parménide* [Paris: Presses Universitaires de France, 1955], p. 56), of which a more literal rendering in English (than that given in the text) is: "The Same, indeed, is at once to think and to be." [*Trans.*]

2. See the preface to the *Phenomenology of the Spirit* (trans. A. V. Miller [Oxford: Oxford University Press, 1977]), especially paragraph 17, which begins as follows: "In my view ... everything turns on grasping and expressing the True [i.e., the Absolute], not only as *Substance*, but equally as *Subject*." [*Trans.*]

3. The third of the syntagms given here in quotation marks, "the unity of a time which endures," does not figure in the passage of Deleuze's text to which Badiou refers. Rather, we find the following syntagm: "a whole which endures." [*Trans.*]

4. This is a quotation from *Ecce Homo*, paragraph 8. [*Trans.*]

5. As noted in chapter 5, translator's note 6, Badiou defines a "situation" as any consistent multiplicity that is presented. In understanding by this that the situation is "what presents the elements that constitute it," one can then proceed to the definition of "the state of the situation" as "what presents, not the situation's elements, but its subsets." The state of a situation thus refers to the order of the subsets of the situation. From this point of view, as Badiou further remarks in the interview with Lauren Sedofsky from which these formulations have been extracted, "the situation is a form of presentation, the state of the situation a form of representation" ("Being by Numbers," Art forum [October 1994]: 87). [*Trans.*]

6. "Eventful" (*événementiel*) is to be understood here (and wherever it appears in this text) in the sense of "having to do with an event." It should be noted, however, that we have translated this term on two previous occasions simply by the noun "event," which therefore accrues an adjectival function. Hence, in the preceding chapter, the expression "event dice throws" in the section titled "Nietzsche or Mallarmé" could also read—in the sense specified—as "eventful dice throws," while the expression "event site," in the preceding paragraph, translates the French *site événementiel*. In this way, our translation of "event site" accords with the translation of this term in the section bearing on Badiou's undertaking in Gilles Deleuze and Félix Guattari's *What Is Philosophy?* (trans. Hugh Tomlinson and Graham Burchell [New York: Columbia University Press, 1994], pp. 151–53), while, on the other hand, the choice of translating "*événementiel*" by "eventful" is one we share with Norman Madarasz in his translation of Badiou's *Manifesto for Philosophy* (Albany: State University of New York Press, 1999). [*Trans.*]

7. The article by Foucault that—inspired by, and bearing on, the work of Maurice Blanchot—has this "expression" (in French: "la pensée du dehors") as its title, has, in fact, been translated into English as "The Thought from Outside" (trans. Brian Massumi, in *Foucault/Blanchot* [New York: Zone Books, 1987], pp. 7–58). However, not only does the translator of Deleuze's *Foucault* employ the preposition "of" in his translations of expressions such as "force of the outside" and "memory of the outside" (trans. Séan Hand [Minneapolis: University of Minnesota Press, 1988], pp. 107 and 113), but, more central to the choice of my translation here, Badiou's next sentence shows that he implicitly understands the preposition *de* in the sense of "of" (and as introducing an "objective"—rather than a "subjective"—complement), for he precisely counsels its suppression in order to do away with any suggestion of an intentional relation between thought and the outside.

Of course, the paradigmatic expression of an intentional relation, in phenomenology—which, as we know, was characterized by Husserl as having intentionality as such for its general theme—is "consciousness-of." [*Trans.*]

8. Badiou quotes here from Mallarmé's poem "Brise Marine"; the French reads as follows: "le vide papier que la blancheur défend." For the English translation, see "Sea Breeze," in Stéphane Mallarmé, *Poems*, trans. Roger Fry (New York: New Directions, 1951). [*Trans.*]

8. A Singularity

1. *vocation*: The French here is *destination*. See chapter 2, translator's note 2. [*Trans.*]

2. In the English translation of Georges Bernanos's *The Diary of a Country Priest* (trans. Pamela Morris, [New York: Carroll and Graf Publishers, (1937) 1983]), these lines are rendered as follows: "Does it matter? Grace is everywhere." [*Trans.*]

3. Léon Brunschvicg (1869–1944): Professor at the Sorbonne from 1909 to 1939, president for many years of the jury for the national qualifying examinations for teachers of philosophy, cofounder of the prestigious *Revue de la métaphysique et de morale*, Brunschvicg was the author of a considerable corpus, which, while elaborating an idealist doctrine, nevertheless sought the eternal of the spirit not in any relationship to the Absolute but in the history of human thought. The major historical references of this "critical idealism" are the Platonic dialectic, the immanentism of Spinoza (unifying science and religion), and, of course, Kant's critical and reflexive method. Defining philosophy as knowledge of knowledge—the intellectual activity's becoming aware of itself—Brunschvicg did not consider philosophy as having for vocation the elaboration of a particular sort of truth; rather, philosophy must affirm scientific activity and disengage from the scientific truth of nature the critical truth of the spirit. [*Trans.*]

4. Albert Lautman (1908–44): Without being a mathematician, Lautman had acquired a profound knowledge of mathematics and, before his premature death (he was executed by the German occupying forces), had concentrated his research on the nature of "mathematical reality." In a session of the French society of philosophy devoted jointly to his and to Jean Cavaillès's dissertations (February 4, 1939), Lautman characterized his reading of Heidegger in the following terms: "The manner in which the Dialectic finds an extension in Mathematics corresponds, it seems to me, to what Heidegger calls the genesis of ontical reality from the ontological analysis of the Idea. One introduces in this way, on the level of the Ideas, an order of the before and after that is not time, but rather, an eternal model of time: the schema of a genesis that is perpetually in process; the necessary order of creation" (*Bulletin de la*

Société française de la philosophie 40 [1946]: 16). The text where this reading of Heidegger is elaborated ("Nouvelles recherches sur la structure dialectique des mathématiques") has been reprinted in *Essais sur l'unité des mathématiques et divers écrits* (Paris: Union Générale des Editions, 1977). [*Trans.*]

5. *historical:* The French here is *historial,* which, as noted in chapter 2, translator's note 3, is the standard rendering in French of the German word *geschichtlich,* in the sense that Heidegger opposes it to *historisch.* [*Trans.*]

"The Univocity of Being"

1. See E. Laroche, *Histoire de la racine nem — en grec ancien* (Paris: Klincksieck, 1949). Laroche shows that the idea of distribution in *nomos-nemò* does not stand in a simple relation to that of allocation (*temnò, diaò, diaireò*). The pastoral sense of *nemò* (to pasture) only belatedly implied an allocation of the land. Homeric society had neither enclosures nor property in pastures: it was not a question of distributing the land among the beasts but, on the contrary, of distributing the beasts themselves and dividing them up here and there across an unlimited space, forest or mountainside. The *nomos* designated first of all an occupied space, but one without precise limits (for example, the expanse around a town) — whence, too, the theme of the "nomad".

"The Virtual"

1. On the correlation between internal milieu and differenciation, see François Meyer, *Problématique de l'évolution* (Paris: Presses Universitaires de France, 1954), pp. 112ff. H. F. Osborn is among those who have most profoundly insisted that life is the posing and solving of 'problems'; mechanical, dynamic or properly biological problems: *The Origin and Evolution of Life: On the Theory of Action, Reaction and Interaction of Energy* (London and New York: G. Bell, 1918). For example, the different types of eye can be studied only in relation to a general physico-biological problem and the variations of its conditions in different animals. The rule governing solutions is that each entails at least one advantage and one drawback.

2. As has already been noted, a couple of lines of Deleuze's original text have been inadvertently omitted in the English translation of *Difference and Repetition.* I have, thus, restored these lines here. See chapter 4, translator's note 3. [*Trans.*]

3. Bergson is the author who pushes furthest the critique of the possible, and also most frequently invokes the notion of the virtual. From *Time and Free-Will,* duration is defined as a non-actual multiplicity (*Time and Free-Will: An Essay on the Immediate Data of Consciousness,* trans. F. L. Pogson [New York: Harper and Row, 1960], p. 84). In *Matter and Memory* (trans. Nancy Margaret Paul and W. Scott Palmer [New York: Zone Books, 1988]), the cone of pure memories with its sections and its 'shining points' on each section (p. 171) is completely real but only virtual. In *Creative Evolution* (trans. Arthur Mitchell [New York: Holt, 1911; reprinted by University Press of America, 1983]), differenciation, or the creation of divergent lines, is understood as an actualisation in which each line of actualisation corresponds to a section of the cone (p. 167).

"Sense and the Task of Philsophy"

1. See Lévi-Strauss' remarks with respect to the "zero-phoneme" in "Introduction à l'oeuvre de Marcel Mauss," in M. Mauss, *Sociologie et anthropologie* (Paris: Presses Universitaires de France, 1950), p. 50.

2. In pages which harmonize with the principal theses of Louis Althusser, J.-P. Osier proposes a distinction between those for whom meaning is to be recovered in a more or less lost origin (whether it be divine or human, ontological or anthropological), and those for whom the origin is a sort of nonsense, for whom meaning is always produced as an epistemological surface effect. Applying this criteria to Marx and Freud, Osier estimates that the problem of interpretation is not at all the problem of going from the "derived" to the "originary", but in comprehending the mechanisms of the production of sense in two series: sense is always an "effect". See preface to Feuerbach's *L'Essence du christianisme* (Paris: Maspero, 1968), especially pp. 15–19.

"The Univocity of Being (II)"

1. On the importance of "empty time" in the elaboration of the event, see B. Groethuysen, "De quelques aspects du temps," *Recherches philosophiques* (1935–1936), vol. 5: "Every event is, so to speak, in time where nothing is happening"; and there is a permanence of empty time spanning everything that happens. The profound interest of Joe Bousquet's book, *Les Capitales,* is that it raised the problem of language in relation to the univocity of Being, beginning with a meditation on Duns Scotus.

"Movement and Multiplicities"

1. On all these points, cf. Henri Bergson, *Matter and Memory,* 1911, chap. 4.

2. *Creative Evolution* [trans. Arthur Mitchell, 1954], p. 10.

3. Ibid., p. 34.

4. Ibid., p. 359.

5. Ibid., p. 16.

6. Ibid. The only resemblance between Bergson and Heidegger — and it is a considerable one — lies here: both base the specificity of time on a conception of the Open.

7. I would signal that I have slightly modified this sentence, for, in the translation of *Cinema 1*, from which this extract comes, the beginning of the sentence is as follows: "It is also inseparable from"; however, the French reads: "Aussi est-elle inséparable de...." [*Trans.*]

8. We raise the problem of relations at this point, although it was not raised explicitly by Bergson. We know that the relation between two things is not reducible to an attribute of one thing or the other, nor, indeed, to an attribute of the set [*ensemble*]. On the other hand, it is still quite possible to relate the relations to a whole [*tout*] if one conceives the whole as a continuum, and not as a given set.

9. *Creative Evolution*, p. 32.

10. Ibid., p. 10.

"Time versus Truth"

1. The word "two" (for the French *deux*), in the phrase "the two following consequences," has mistakenly been replaced by the word "true" in the English edition of *Cinema 2* from which this passage has been extracted. [*Trans.*]

2. Cf.: P. M. Schuhl, *Le Dominateur et les possibles*, PUF (on the role of this paradox in Greek philosophy). Jules Vuillemin has taken up the whole question in *Nécessité ou contingence*, Minuit.

3. Cf.: Leibniz, *Theodicy*, sections 414–16; in this astonishing text, which we consider a source of all modern literature, Leibniz presents 'contingent futures' as so many compartments making up a pyramid of crystal. In one compartment Sextus does not go to Rome and cultivates his garden in Corinth; in another he becomes king in Thrace; but in another, he goes to Rome and takes power ... It will be noticed that this text is presented in a very complex and inextricable narration, even though it presumes to save the Truth; it is first a dialogue between Valla and Antony, in which is inserted another dialogue between Sextus and the oracle of Apollo, then this is succeeded by a third dialogue, Sextus and Jupiter, which gives way to the Theodorus and Pallus discussion at the end of which Theodorus wakes up.

4. Borges, 'The garden with forking paths,' in *Labyrinths*, trans. Donald A. Yates (Harmondsworth: Penguin, 1970).

"The Thought of the Outside"

1. See *L'Usage des plaisirs* [Paris: Gallimard, 1984], p. 15; (*The Use of Pleasure* [trans. Robert Hurley (New York: Random House, 1985, and Harmondsworth: Viking, 1986)], p. 9). The most profound study of Foucault, history and conditions is by Paul Veyne, 'Foucault revolutionizes history,' in *Comment on écrit l'histoire* (Paris: Seuil, 1971), especially on the question of 'invariants'.

2. The trinity of Nietzsche, Mallarmé and Artaud is invoked above all at the end of *The Order of Things* [trans. Allan Sheridan (London: Tavistock and New York: Pantheon, 1970)].

3. See *L'Ordre du discours* [Paris: Gallimard, 1971], p. 37, where Foucault invokes a 'wild exteriority' and offers the example of Mendel, who dreamed up biological objects, concepts and methods that could not be assimilated by the biology of his day. This does not at all contradict the idea that there is no wild experience. It does not exist, because any experience already supposes knowledge and power-relations. Therefore for this very reason wild singularities find themselves pushed out of knowledge and power into the 'margins,' so much so that science cannot recognize them. See *L'Ordre du discours*, pp. 35–37.

4. Husserl himself invoked in thought a 'fiat' like the throw of a dice or the positions of a point in his *Ideen zu einer reinen Phänomenologie und phänomenologischen Philosophie* (1913).

5. *Les Mots et les choses* [Paris: Gallimard, 1966], p. 338; (*The Order of Things* [trans. Allan Sheridan (London: Tavistock and New York: Pantheon, 1970)], p. 327). See also the commentary on Husserl's phenomenology, *Les Mots et les choses*, p. 336 (*The Order of Things*, p. 325).

6. See G. Simondon, *L'Individu et sa genèse physico-biologique* (Paris: Presses Universitaires de France, 1964), pp. 258–65.

Index

nonrelation, 22–23, 25, 65; with regard to relation, 83, 84, 86, 88, 89
nonsense (*see also* sense), 11, 38–40, 75
number, 4, 21, 24, 37, 48

One (*see also* Being, One-All), 35, 43, 80, 91, 95, 97, 98, 99, 100; author's disqualification of, 4, 46, 52–53, 64; Being as, 20–28, 45, 52, 79, 83; beings as modalities of, 36, 44, 81; Deleuze's renewed concept of, 10–14, 17; and disjunction, 84–90; equivalence with multiplicities, 56; and the eternal return, 68–76; identified with life, 38–39; identified with the virtual, 48–49, 51–52, 59, 61; and intuition, 40; and Plato, 46, 58; and time, 62–65
One-All (*see also* All, whole), 2, 11–13, 24, 37
ontology, 23, 69, 76, 80, 82, 85, 87, 89; identified with philosophy, 20, 24; Mallarmé, 72; and univocity, 25–26, 28–29, 31–32, 34, 38–40, 43, 47, 73–74
Open, 9, 37, 68, 71, 98, 101; Bergson and, 49, 62, 99; Heidegger and, 21, 23
outside, 14, 21, 29, 68, 71, 81, 86–91; and choice, 12; memory of, 65; "thought of," 86; and void, 85

Parmenides, 20, 33, 68, 76, 79, 102
passivity. *See* activity
phenomenology, 4, 16, 19, 20–21, 23, 47, 59, 81, 87, 98
philosophy 19, 53, 55, 58, 60, 67, 69, 76, 84, 95, 102; characterization of Deleuze's, 2, 13–14, 16–17, 20, 23–24, 29, 33, 45–46, 62, 73, 91; Deleuze's genealogy of, 24, 100–101; "end of," 5, 101; in France, 3–4, 96–98; identified with ontology, 20, 23–24; thinking of thought, 21, 79; of subject, 12, 80–82
physicists, 102
Plato: *Parmenides*, 27, 57; *Republic*, 27, 58; *Sophist*, 31, 67; *Timaeus*, 70
Platonism, 1, 28, 33, 48, 64, 65, 80, 98–99; Deleuzianism as, 26, 32, 46, 61; division of Being, 31–32, 35, 84; mimetic vision of Being, 43–45; overturning of, 9, 14, 17, 26, 27, 45, 101; restoration of, 101–2; the Same, 67, 70, 74; truth, 57–58
Proust, Marcel, 10, 14

real, 26, 44, 57, 71, 72, distinction with formal, 25, 27–28; opposed to possible, 11, 48–49, 51; virtual as, 46–47, 49–53, 56, 85;
reconcatenation, 36, 51, 83, 84
Relation (*see also* nonrelation), 63–65, 68, 83, 89
repetition, 10, 14–16, 24, 36, 69, 72, 83
Riemann, Georg, 24

Sacher-Masoch, 10, 15, 28
Same, 22, 44–45, 57, 67–74, 76, 79, 83, 97
Sartre, Jean-Paul, 1, 21, 81, 98; *Critique of Dialectical Reason*, 98

sense (*see also* nonsense), 89; equivocity and, 23, 32–33, 48, 69, 73, 81; logic of, 9, 75; structuralism, 37, 38; univocity, 20, 24–29, 34–35, 39–40, 46, 49, 79
sets, 1; objects as, in opposition to whole, 39, 63, 83–85, 97–98; paradigm of multiple, 4, 46–48
simulacr(a)um, 29, 46, 86; modalities of Being, 33–36, 38–40, 44, 48–49, 51–52, 55, 59, 61–62, 69, 71, 73–74, 80–81, 83–85, 88; multiple, 11, 26, 28, 56, 71; Platonism, 26–27, 32, 43–44, 57, 61; structuralism, 37–38
singularities, 9, 12–13, 15, 33, 91
situation, 64, 75, 76, 85
Spinoza, Baruch, 13–15, 28, 33, 40, 53, 97; importance for Deleuze, 1, 15, 39, 100–102; univocity, 24–25
Stoics, 1, 4, 13, 24, 97, 99, 100–101
structuralism, 36–39, 98
subject, 23, 29, 65, 68–69, 80–83, 90

Tarde, Gabriel, 10
Teilhard de Chardin, Pierre, 99
Théorie du sujet, 3
thinking (*see also* intuition), 9, 26, 31, 45; and being, 20–21, 35–40, 79–91; conditions of, 12–17; destination of, 11, 15; symbolized by death, 14; as "throw of the dice," 29
time, 21, 26, 100; author's interpretation of, 60, 64–65; Bergson and, 15, 52, 61–63, 83, 98; in cinema, 15–16, 87–88; of eternal return, 70, 72, 74; and memory, 90; and movement, 15–16; and name of Being, 83, 90; and truth, 29, 55, 59–65, 67; as whole of relations, 63–64
topology, 87–88
transcendence, 14, 27, 46, 56, 80, 91, 100–101
truth, 9, 47, 84, 86, 88; author's interpretation of, 3, 55, 58, 60, 64–65, 75–76, 92; as category, 56–57; as memory, 64–65, 67; as power of the false, 57–59; and time, 29, 55, 59–65, 67

undecidable, 57–58, 75
univocity. *See* Being; One

virtual and virtualization (*see also* actual), 13, 33, 40, 81, 97, 100, 102; author's critique of, 51–53, 65, 76, 85, 91–92; eternal return of, 69, 73, 75; function as ground of, 46–53, 63; as memory, 64–65, 91; and names of Being, 29, 43, 48, 59, 62, 79; reality of, 49, 55; in relation to truth, 56, 58, 61–62, 64–65
void, 11, 45, 53, 76, 85, 89, 91

Wahl, François, 4
Whitehead, Alfred N., 10, 15, 100
whole (*see also* All, One-All), 40, 49, 51, 62–65, 85, 88
Wittgenstein, Ludwig, 19, 20, 83; *Tractatus*, 19

Alain Badiou teaches philosophy at the University of Paris-VIII (Vincennes-Saint Denis) and at the Collège international de philosophie in Paris. Trained in mathematics as well as philosophy, and inspired by psychoanalysis, he is also a playwright and novelist.

Louise Burchill teaches at the Collège international de philosophie in Paris. She attended Gilles Deleuze's courses from 1981 to 1987. Her publications include articles on "the feminine" in contemporary French philosophy and translations of work by Julia Kristeva.